the HAIRY BIKERS' FAMILY COOKBOOK

Mums know best!
xxx

Tessa

Peter & Susan

Gameelah

Maureen

Jennie & Bridget

Eele

Connie

Fiona

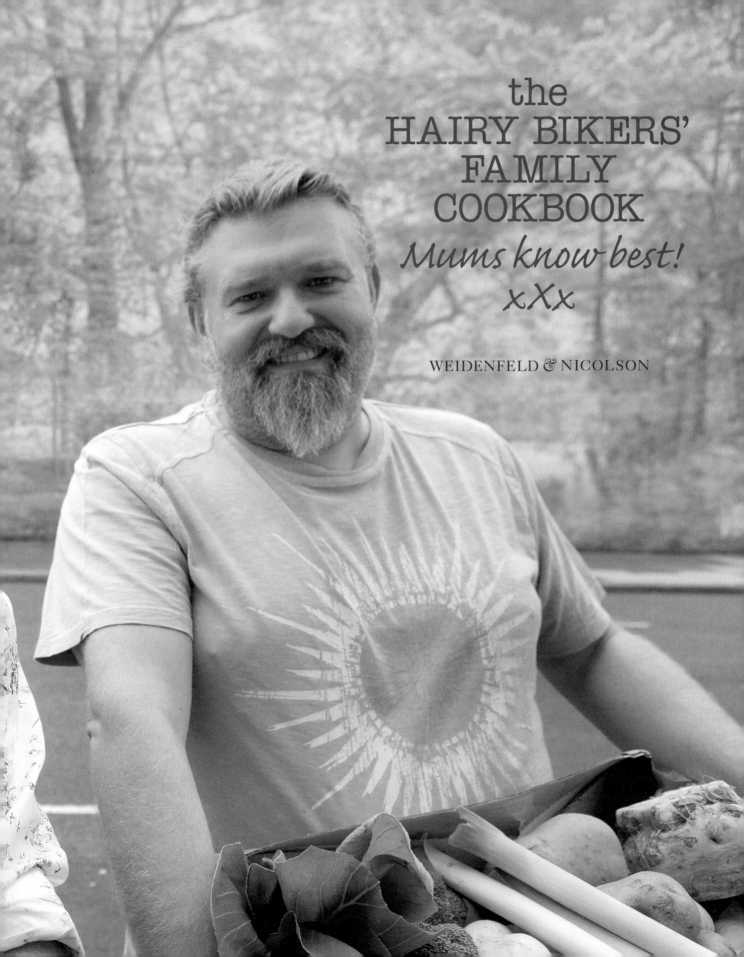

the
HAIRY BIKERS'
FAMILY
COOKBOOK

Mums know best!
xXx

WEIDENFELD & NICOLSON

We dedicate this book to our mams,
Stella & **Margaret**, without whom it
would not have been possible. And
to mums everywhere – the world
can't exist without you.

First published in hardback in Great Britain in 2010 by
Orion Books an imprint of the Orion Publishing Group Ltd
Orion House, 5 Upper St Martin's Lane, London WC2H 9EA
an Hachette UK Company

14

Text copyright © Simon King and Dave Myers 2010
Design and layout copyright © Weidenfeld & Nicolson 2010

A CIP catalogue record for this book is available from the British Library.

ISBN: 978 0 29786 026 6

Photography by Cristian Barnett
Designed by Kate Barr
Edited by Jinny Johnson
Proofread by Elise See Tai
Index by Elizabeth Wiggans

Printed in Italy

The Orion Publishing Group's policy is to use papers that are natural, renewable and recyclable and made
from wood grown in sustainable forests. The logging and manufacturing processes are expected to conform
to the environmental regulations of the country of origin.

www.orionbooks.co.uk

There's nothing better than sitting round the table with your nearest and dearest and enjoying a good meal.

Cooking is a huge part of family life and in every family, who knows best? Mum, of course! We learned lots of our favourite recipes from our own mums and we still cook and enjoy these dishes with our families today. All our favourites are included here – roast beef, fishcakes, blackberry and apple pie and other classics, as well as our own twists on new family treats, such as samosas and chicken Maryland.

Looking at our family recipes got us thinking and made us want to find out what secrets and treasures the nation's mums have hidden in their family recipe books and apron pockets. We invited everyone to tell us about their favourites and the response was fantastic. We've met so many great mums who've shared their family dishes with us and told us about their cooking traditions from many different heritages that have been handed down through generations. The best are in this book – fantastic feasts like Texas cornbread, Caribbean curried mutton, an Estonian pudding and a wealth of wonderful Indian curries.

We also organised some Recipe Fairs up and down the country and invited everyone and anyone to come along with family recipes, cooked dishes, favourite cooking tools and tips. We couldn't believe how many people turned up and shared their family favourites, including community groups such as the Bradford Curry Project, the WI and even some soldiers from a Gurkha regiment! We all had a cracking time and learned a lot about what families in Britain today like to eat.

All the recipes in this book are served up with a huge ladleful of love. They are dishes that we will cook time and time again and we hope you will too.

love Si & Dave

Family
favourites

BEER-BATTERED FISH

To make good battered fish, you need really fresh fish and oil at the perfect temperature to cook the batter. If the oil temperature is right, the fish will steam inside, forcing the fat out, and the batter will be super-light and crispy.

SERVES 4

1½ –2 litres sunflower oil,
for deep frying
4 tbsp plain flour
½ tsp fine sea salt
4 x 200g thick white fish fillets,
such as haddock or cod

BATTER
75g cornflour
200g plain flour
1 tsp fine sea salt
330ml bottle of real ale
2 tbsp white wine vinegar

First make the batter. Mix the cornflour, plain flour and salt together in a large bowl. Make a well in the centre and stir in the ale and vinegar. Beat with a large metal whisk to make a smooth batter. It should have the consistency of double cream.

Half fill a large deep saucepan with sunflower oil and heat the oil to 180ºC. It's important to use a cooking thermometer and check the temperature regularly. Do not allow the oil to overheat and never leave the hot oil unattended. (Alternatively, use an electric deep-fat fryer heated to 180ºC.)

Put the flour in a large plastic food bag and season with the salt. Add the fish fillets, one at a time, and shake to coat them in the seasoned flour.

When the oil has reached the right temperature, stir the batter well. Take one floured fish fillet and dip it in the batter until it is thoroughly coated. Lift it out with some tongs and gently drop it into the hot oil. Watch out for splashes as the oil will be extremely hot.

Do the same with a second fish fillet and cook it with the first for 5–6 minutes, depending on the thickness of the fillet, or until golden and crisp. Make sure the batter doesn't brown too quickly leaving the fish uncooked. Transfer the fish to a plate lined with kitchen paper to absorb any excess oil. Reheat the oil and cook the next two pieces of fish in exactly the same way. Serve with freshly cooked chips.

In fact, you can cook the fish in the same oil as the chips. Cook the fish after giving the chips their first fry, then keep the fish warm while you finish the chips.

THE BEST CHIPS EVER

The secret of good chips is to cook them twice at two different temperatures, so you will need a deep pan and a thermometer for this recipe.

SERVES 4

4 large floury potatoes
2 litres sunflower oil, for deep frying
sea salt
malt vinegar

For the best chips, always use floury potatoes with a good fibre content – that is, more potato and less water. Yukon Gold, Nadine and Maris Piper are all great, or try Cyprus if you're feeling flush.

Peel the potatoes and cut them into slices roughly 1cm thick. Cut each slice into fairly thick chips and rinse them in a colander under plenty of cold water to remove excess starch. (If you have time, it's worth letting the chips soak in a bowl of cold water for several hours or overnight.) Blot them dry on kitchen paper.

Half fill a large deep saucepan with sunflower oil and heat to 130°C. It's important to use a cooking thermometer and check the temperature regularly. Do not allow the oil to overheat and never leave hot oil unattended. (We've learned that the fire brigade are dead against this method of deep frying so if possible, get yourself an electric deep-fat fryer.)

Gently drop half the chips into the hot oil and stir carefully with a large metal spoon. Leave to fry for 10 minutes until cooked through but not browned. Remove the chips with a slotted spoon and drain on plenty of kitchen paper. Follow the same method with the rest of the chips and drain well. (The chips can be left for several hours at this stage.)

When ready to serve, reheat the oil to 190°C. Lower all the chips gently into the pan and cook for 4–5 minutes until crisp and golden brown. Lift them out with a slotted spoon and drain on kitchen paper. Tip into a serving dish and sprinkle with salt and vinegar to serve.

MINCED MEAT PLATE PIE

We have wonderful memories of this sort of pie, which both our mothers used to make – Dave's mam used to crimp the edges of the pastry with her false teeth! This really is a cut-and-come-again pie. You think you'll just have one more bit and suddenly there isn't enough left to feed a sparrow.

MAKES A PIE FOR A LARGE DINNER PLATE

FILLING

750g good-quality minced beef
2 onions, diced
1 beef stock cube
400ml boiling water
salt and pepper to taste,
(heavy on the pepper)
butter, for greasing the plate
1 egg, beaten, for sealing the edge
and glazing the top crust

SHORTCRUST PASTRY

450g plain flour
2 tsp baking powder
½ tsp salt
60g unsalted butter, diced
60g lard, diced
1 egg yolk

First make the pastry. Briefly mix the flour, baking powder and salt in a food processor. Add the butter, lard and egg yolk and process until the mixture forms crumbs. Gradually add up to 120ml of cold water until a ball of pastry miraculously appears. Alternatively, struggle on with a basin, your fingers and a spoon. Wrap the pastry in clingfilm and leave it to chill in the fridge for an hour so it's easier to roll out.

Meanwhile, make the filling. This is Si's mam's method and it worked for several decades, so give it a go. Preheat the oven to 180°C/Gas 4. Mix the mince with the onions in a casserole dish. Dissolve the beef stock cube in the water and pour this over the meat. Season well, going heavy on the pepper. Put the lid on the casserole dish and cook in the preheated oven for 30 minutes.

Then, take the lid off and leave the meat to cook until most of the liquid has evaporated and the flavour has developed. This will take about another 30 minutes. Remove from the oven and leave to cool.

Preheat the oven to 180°C/Gas 4. Grease the dinner plate with a splodge of butter. Roll out half the pastry and line the plate, then add the meat filling, leaving a good rim of pastry. Brush the edges of the pastry with the beaten egg. Roll out the rest of the pastry to make the lid and cover the meat, sealing the edges together well. Cut a couple of slashes in the pastry lid to let out the steam, brush with beaten egg and bake for about 30 minutes until the pastry is golden.

CHEESE PIE

Maureen Kirkland lives outside Glasgow. She learned to cook from her mum, taught her own children and now loves to cook with her grandchildren. This cheesy mash was a dish she always made when her children were poorly – it's real comfort food and a proper family tradition.

SERVES 6

700g potatoes
butter and milk
white pepper
550g mature white cheese, grated
55g fresh breadcrumbs

Peel the potatoes, cut them into chunks and boil in slightly salted water until soft. Drain well and mash with a large knob of butter and a little milk. Season with ground white pepper – white tastes better in mash than black. Add about one-third of the grated cheese and mix it in well. Preheat the oven to 180°C/Gas 4.

Now you need an ovenproof dish, about 5–7.5cm deep. Add half the mashed potato and top with half the remaining cheese. Season with more pepper and add the rest of the potato. Mix the rest of the cheese with the breadcrumbs and sprinkle over the top of the potato. Bake in the oven for 25–30 minutes until crisp and golden on top. Serve with some seasonal vegetables.

One variation is to soften a finely chopped onion in a small amount of olive oil and add this to the potato/cheese mixture. Or, 10 minutes before the end of the cooking time, top with a couple of sliced tomatoes.

CHILLI CON CARNE

When Maureen's children were little she used to cook a dish they always called beany mince – basically a way of eeking out a bit of meat, but they loved it. As the children grew up and their tastes changed, the recipe got spicier and spicier until it evolved into a full-on chilli and now they all cook their own versions. This is the recipe Barry, Maureen's son, makes. And below is the beany mince where it all started.

SERVES 2

1 tbsp vegetable oil
250g minced beef
1 large onion, peeled and finely chopped
1 green and 1 red pepper, seeded and chopped
dash of Worcestershire sauce
2 small bird's eye chillies, chopped
couple of splashes of Tabasco sauce
1 x 400g can of chopped tomatoes
2 tbsp tomato purée
1 beef stock cube
2 limes
1–2 tbsp ground cumin
handful of fresh coriander, chopped
1 x 400g can of red kidney beans

Heat the oil in a large pan with a lid. Brown the beef, then add the onion, peppers, Worcestershire sauce, chillies, Tabasco, tomatoes and tomato purée. Crumble in the stock cube and add the juice of 1 lime and some ground cumin – start with one spoonful, taste and add another if you like. Season with salt and pepper and add a little of the chopped coriander.

Cover and simmer until the meat is ready – it will take about 45 minutes to an hour. Stir in the kidney beans and cook until they are warmed through, then add lots more chopped coriander. Garnish with extra chillies if you like. Wipe the serving dish with the juice of half a lime and serve with some lime slices. Dish up with rice or on top of lightly salted tortilla chips, open a cold beer and book a fire engine!

BEANY MINCE

And this is the junior version. Maureen serves it with pasta, rice, mash or wraps and some more veg – whatever's in the cupboard.

SERVES 3–4

1 tsp vegetable oil
225g minced beef
1 onion, peeled and finely chopped
110g carrots, finely chopped or grated
30–60g turnip or swede, peeled and finely chopped
1 generous tbsp tomato purée
1 x 415g can of baked beans

Heat the oil in a large pan with a lid. Brown the mince, then add the chopped onion and continue cooking until it has softened. Add the carrots and turnip or swede with up to 150ml boiling water. Don't add it all at once, as too much water makes the final dish sloppy. You can always add more if you need it.

Cover the pan and cook until the meat and veggies are done, then add the tomato purée and baked beans (including the liquid). Continue to cook until everything is heated through. Season lightly before serving.

RUMPY-PUMPY SOUP

Maureen used to make this red lentil soup for her children as a way of getting them to eat more veg without any fuss – she'd liquidise the soup so that they didn't know what was in it. Now, though, she prefers to leave the vegetables in chunks or she mashes them down with a potato masher. And in case you're wondering, in Maureen's family, rumpy-pumpy doesn't mean what you think it does. Her dad named the soup because of the well-known effects of lentils – they make you trump!

SERVES 6

about 2 litres ham stock
450g carrots, peeled and chopped
225g turnip or swede peeled and chopped
340g onions, finely chopped
any other 'secret' veggies, such as sprouts,
leeks, finely chopped cabbage, even a can
of chopped tomatoes
225g red lentils
salt and pepper

Best to make the stock the night before with a ham bone or hock so the flavour can develop.

Cook the vegetables in the ham stock until soft, then add the lentils. Stir frequently at this stage, as lentils can burn quite easily. If you have made the stock with a ham hock, remove any meat, chop it and add to the soup. Season to taste.

Maureen sometimes adds chunks of potato to cook in the soup to make it more filling, or stirs in 1–2 teaspoons of ground cumin to give it a curry flavour.

YELLOW SPLIT PEA & HAM SOUP

And here's our version. Make a big pan of this and let it moulder on for days.
It will taste better and better.

SERVES 6

2 tbsp vegetable oil
2 onions, peeled and diced
1 ham knuckle
500g yellow split peas
2 bay leaves
chopped parsley
salt and pepper

Heat the oil in a big pan. Add the onions and sweat until translucent, then add the ham knuckle, split peas, bay leaves, lots of pepper and a little salt. Go easy with the salt until the end because the knuckle will give out a lot of salt. Pour in about 2 litres of water and bring everything to the boil.

Simmer gently, skimming the scum off as necessary, for about 2 hours. By this time, the peas will have 'dropped' – that is, gone all mushy. Remove the knuckle and as soon as it is cool enough, shred off the meat and add it to the soup.

Put the bone back in too, reheat the soup and check the seasoning. Serve with crusty bread and parsley sprinkles if the vicar is coming for his tea.

When you have stripped the meat from the bone, put the bone back in the soup to steep and enrich the flavours.

TANDOORI CHICKEN SAMOSAS

This is a fantastic recipe we got off a fella we met on a train in Goa.
He swore blind that his mother used to make it all the time. It might look like a lot of work
but you can make the filling in advance and then fill and cook the samosas when you're ready.
Dead easy really and well worth it. Give it a go and spice up your life.

MAKES 10–12

FILLING

1 tbsp tandoori paste
1 tbsp yoghurt
2 chicken breasts
2 medium potatoes, peeled
2 tbsp vegetable oil
1 small onion, very finely diced
½ tsp ground turmeric
2 tsp garam masala
1 tsp mustard seeds
½ tsp ground black pepper
1 tsp salt
4 cloves garlic, crushed
1 green chilli (or half if you don't like
things too hot!)
10 curry leaves
75g frozen peas
1 tsp lemon juice
handful of coriander leaves, chopped
more vegetable oil, for deep frying

Mix the tandoori paste with the yoghurt. Put the chicken breasts in a bowl, cover them with the yoghurt mixture and leave in the fridge to marinate for an hour.

Meanwhile, make the pastry. Place the flour in a bowl and stir in the salt. Work in the oil and the egg yolk until the mixture has a crumb-like texture. (Keep the egg white for later when you assemble the samosas.)

Gradually mix in the warm (blood-temperature) water to form a stiff elastic dough, adding more or less water to get a workable texture. Wrap the dough in clingfilm and put it in the fridge to chill while you make the filling.

Preheat the oven to 190°C/Gas 5. Put the marinated chicken in a baking dish and bake in the oven for about 20 minutes or until just cooked through. Leave to cool, then chop into tiny chunks. All of this can be done ahead of time if you like.

Boil the potatoes whole for about 15 minutes or until tender. Drain and set them aside to cool, then dice finely.

Heat the 2 tablespoons of oil in a frying pan and sweat the onion until soft but not brown. Add the turmeric, garam masala, mustard seeds, black pepper and salt and cook for a minute. Then add the garlic and chilli and sauté for another 2 minutes. Add the curry leaves to the pan and cook for a further minute.

PASTRY
250g plain flour
1 tsp salt
1 dsrtsp vegetable oil
1 egg, separated
9 tbsp warm water

Add the diced potato and mix well, but gently, into the spices and cook over a low heat for another 10 minutes to release all the flavours into the potatoes. Add the peas and cook gently for 2–3 minutes. Finally, fold in the chicken, add the lemon juice and chopped coriander and check the seasoning. Set the filling aside to get cold.

ASSEMBLING THE SAMOSAS
Roll out the pastry to about 3mm – not too thin, but not too thick. Take a side plate and press it onto the pastry to make an impression. Cut round the impression with a knife to make a circle, then cut this in half. Take one half and make a cone. Make sure the edges of the cone overlap, then use your fingers to squash the edges gently together to seal them.

Spoon the filling into the cone until it is about three-quarters full – do not overfill. Brush the top edge with egg white and, using your fingers, pinch the edges together to seal in the filling. Repeat until you have used up all the filling.

Heat the oil to a gentle rumble and deep fry the samosas for about 5 minutes until they are golden and crunchy. Serve with some chutney and raita.

TRADITIONAL SAMOSAS

Gameelah Ghafoor from Dundee cooked us some amazing food. Her dad is from Yemen and her mother is Scottish, so she grew up eating food from both traditions. Dad's specialities were curries and samosas, while mum showed her how to make stovies and stews. Gameelah has brought both cultures together to create family favourites in her own special style. Her dad has a neat trick with samosas. Instead of making pastry, he uses tortillas to wrap the filling and this is the way Gameelah cooked them for us.

2 tbsp vegetable oil, such as sunflower
1 onion, peeled and finely chopped
½ tsp chopped garlic
½ tsp grated root ginger
1 tsp cumin seeds
1 tsp coriander seeds
1 rounded tbsp curry paste (any kind)
1 tsp garam masala
500g minced beef
1 potato, peeled and diced small
16 tortillas
1 egg, beaten, to seal the tortilla

Heat the oil in a large frying pan and add the chopped onion. Once the onion is soft, add the garlic and ginger. Grind the cumin and coriander seeds and add them to the pan with the curry paste and garam masala. Fry this mixture for 2 minutes, then add the mince. Once the mince is browned, add the diced potato and pour in a little boiling water to allow the potato to cook. Let everything simmer until the potato is soft and the water has reduced.

Cut the tortillas in half, then cut each half into long strips the width of four fat fingers. Put the smaller side of the tortilla next to you and place your finger in the middle of the bottom side. Keeping your finger in place, diagonally fold over the bottom right side to the top to make a kite shape. Do the same with the other side. Brush egg onto the folds of the tortilla to help the sides stick together. Lift up the tortilla and make a cone shape, then add some filling.

Lay the filled tortilla down, brush the flap at the top with beaten egg and fold it over to make a triangle. Turn it flap-side down on the work surface and gently press to seal. Pinch the points of the tortilla to make sure the filling does not come out. Continue filling tortillas in the same way until all the mixture is used up.

Heat some oil in a large pan or deep-fat fryer to about 160°C if the filling is cold and to 180°C if the filling is already hot. Fry the samosas for a couple of minutes, turning them once, until they are golden brown on each side. Don't overcrowd the pan – just cook 3 or 4 at a time. Eat and enjoy!

VEGGIE SAMOSAS

This is a favourite variation in Gameelah's household.

1 tbsp sunflower oil
½ onion, peeled and finely diced
½ tsp chopped garlic
¼ tsp turmeric
¼ tsp chilli flakes
100g mushrooms, chopped
100g peeled prawns
100g petit pois
1 red pepper, finely diced
100g rice
soy sauce, to taste

Heat the oil in a saucepan and fry the onion and garlic until softened. Stir in the turmeric and chilli flakes and fry for another 2 minutes. Then add the mushrooms, prawns, peas and red pepper and continue to cook for 2 minutes.

Stir in the rice. Add about 250ml of hot water, bring to the boil and cover the pan. Simmer over a low heat until the rice is done. Splash on some soy sauce and use this mixture to fill the samosas as before.

OTHER FILLINGS TO TRY

Haggis

Mushroom risotto

Prawn, spinach, onion, garlic, ginger and chilli

Chickpea, spinach, onion, garlic, chilli, cumin, coriander

Black pudding

MINCE & DUMPLINGS

This is something we both loved as kids – and still do. If you want
your dumplings golden, take the lid off the pan 10 minutes before the end
of the cooking time so that they crisp up, or finish them off under the grill

SERVES 6

2 tbsp sunflower oil
1 large onion, halved and thinly sliced
2 garlic cloves, peeled
and finely chopped
2 celery sticks, stringed
and finely sliced
2 medium carrots, peeled and diced
500g lean minced beef
1 x 400g can of chopped tomatoes
2 tbsp tomato purée
350ml beef stock (fresh or from a cube)
150ml red wine
pinch of caster sugar
1 bay leaf
salt and freshly ground black pepper

DUMPLINGS
250g self-raising flour
125g shredded beef suet
½ tsp fine sea salt
2 tbsp finely chopped fresh parsley

Heat the oil in a large saucepan or flameproof casserole
dish. Cook the onion, garlic, celery and carrots for
15 minutes, stirring occasionally, until they begin to
soften and lightly colour. Add the beef and cook with
the vegetables for another 5 minutes until the mince
is no longer pink. Stir regularly to break up the meat.

Add the tomatoes, tomato puree, beef stock, red wine,
sugar and bay leaf. Season with a good pinch of salt and
plenty of black pepper. Bring to the boil, then reduce the
heat and simmer gently for 20 minutes, stirring occasionally.

To make the dumplings, put the flour in a bowl and stir
in the suet, salt and parsley. Make a well in the centre and
add enough cold water – you'll need about 200ml – to make
a soft, spongy dough. Lightly flour your hands and roll the
dumpling mixture into 12 small balls.

Stir the mince well and remove it from the heat. Drop
the dumplings carefully on top of the mince. Cover with
a tight-fitting lid and return to a medium heat. Cook for
18–20 minutes or until the dumplings are well risen
and light.

BOILED LEEK & ONION PUDDING
WITH COLD CUTS & GRAVY

This is Si's mam's recipe for a mid-week family filler. Fantastic with cold cuts and leftover gravy.

SERVES 6

25g butter, plus extra for greasing
1 tbsp sunflower oil
1 medium onion, finely chopped
2 slender leeks, trimmed
and finely sliced
150g fresh white breadcrumbs
200g self-raising flour, plus
extra for dusting
115g shredded beef suet
1 heaped tsp fine sea salt
freshly ground black pepper
1 large free-range egg
75ml whole milk
cold roast meat and hot gravy, to serve

Melt the butter with the oil in a large frying pan. Gently fry the onion and leeks for 5 minutes or until well softened, stirring regularly. Remove from the heat and set them aside to cool for a few minutes.

Mix the breadcrumbs, flour, suet, salt and plenty of freshly ground black pepper in a large bowl. Stir in the onion and leeks. Beat together the egg and milk. Stir into the dry ingredients until well combined – the dough should feel light and spongy. Turn the dough out onto a floured board, knead very lightly and form into a large ball.

Half fill a large saucepan with water and bring to the boil. Sprinkle flour liberally over a large piece of clean sheeting, or a thin drying-up cloth. (An old pillow case can also be cut to size for this job.) Place the pudding on the sheet and gather up the sides. Leave room for expansion, then tie tightly with kitchen string to seal the parcel.

Lower the pudding gently and carefully into the boiling water, cover with a lid and boil for 1 hour. By this time, the pudding should be well risen and light. Check the water level now and then while it's boiling and top up if necessary. (Alternatively, put the pudding in a 1.5-litre basin lined with buttered baking parchment. Cover with pleated parchment and foil and tie it tightly with string. Steam the pudding on a trivet in a deep saucepan half filled with boiling water for about 2 hours.)

Turn off the heat and lift the pudding carefully from the water using tongs. Take great care as the water will be very hot. Put the pudding on a board and leave it to cool for a few minutes before snipping off the string and transferring the pud to a serving dish. Serve in wedges with cold roast meat and a jug of steaming hot gravy.

STEAK & KIDNEY PUDDING

We agree that a proper steak and kidney pudding is one of life's great pleasures –
a real family treat. Just make sure you trim the meat carefully and core and trim
the kidneys so you don't have any nasty chewy bits spoiling your fun.

SERVES 6

700g braising steak, well marbled
with fat
3 very fresh lambs' kidneys
3 tbsp plain flour
4–5 tbsp sunflower oil
1 medium onion, chopped
200ml red wine
4–5 sprigs of fresh thyme
1 bay leaf
500ml good beef stock
1 tbsp tomato purée
fine sea salt and black pepper

SUET PASTRY

350g self-raising flour
175g shredded suet
½ tsp fine sea salt
butter, for greasing

Trim the beef of any thick fat or tough bits of gristle and cut into cubes of about 2.5cm. Rinse the kidneys and pat them dry with kitchen paper. Snip out the white cores and cut the kidneys into 1.5cm chunks. Put the steak and kidneys in a large, strong plastic bag. Add the flour, salt and plenty of black pepper. Knot the top of the bag and shake until the meat is well coated in the seasoned flour. Preheat the oven to 170°C/Gas 3.

Heat 2 tablespoons of the oil in a large non-stick frying pan and fry the steak and kidneys over a medium heat until well browned all over. You'll need to do this in a few batches so you don't overcrowd the pan, so add an extra tablespoon or two of oil if the pan gets dry. Transfer the meat to a flameproof casserole dish as it is browned. Return the pan to the heat and add the remaining oil, then the onion. Cook over a low heat for 5 minutes or until softened, stirring often. Stir the onion into the casserole dish with the steak and kidneys.

Deglaze the frying pan with the wine, bringing it to the boil while stirring hard to lift all the sediment from the bottom of the pan. Pour immediately over the meat and onions. Strip the thyme leaves from the stalks and add them to the casserole dish. Stir in the bay leaf, beef stock and tomato purée. Bring everything to the boil, then cover and cook in the oven for 1½–2 hours or until the meat is tender. Give it a stir halfway through the cooking time. Take out 3 ladlefuls of the sauce and set aside to use for gravy later – once cool, this can be kept in the fridge until needed.

When the meat is done, take the dish out of the oven and place it on the hob. Simmer, uncovered, for 2–3 minutes or until the sauce is thick enough to coat the beef generously. The sauce needs to be thick enough not to run out over the plate when the pudding is cut, but not too thick or the pudding will taste dry. Take off the heat and leave to cool.

A nice touch is to mix 2 teaspoons of dried mixed herbs into the suet pastry. As the pud steams, they will give the suet crust a lovely herby flavour.

To make the suet pastry, put the flour in a large bowl and stir in the suet and salt. Stir in enough water to make soft, spongy dough – you'll probably need about 300ml. Turn the dough out onto a floured surface and bring it together to form a ball. Knead lightly, then remove a generous quarter of the dough to make a lid for the pudding and roll the rest into a circle measuring about 25cm (the size of an average dinner plate). It should be about 1cm thick.

Use this to line a well-buttered 1.5-litre pudding basin with the pastry level resting at about 1cm below the top edge of the dish. Press well against the sides of the basin and trim neatly, then pile in the cooled steak and kidney mixture. Brush the top edge of the pastry with water. Roll the remaining pastry into a round just large enough to sit on top of the pastry edge and place over the filling. Trim into place and press the edges together to seal.

Cover the dish with a large circle of baking parchment, with a pleat in the middle to allow for expansion. Cover the parchment with a circle of foil, again with a pleat. Tie both tightly in place with string. Create a carrying handle by tying the excess string across the top of the basin – this will help you lift the pudding once it's cooked.

Place on an upturned saucer or a small trivet in a large deep saucepan and add enough just-boiled water to come halfway up the sides of the basin. (Alternatively, cook in a hob-top steamer.) Cover the pan with a tight-fitting lid and place over a medium heat. Allow to steam in simmering water for 2½ hours, adding more hot water when necessary.

When the pudding is done, turn off the heat and carefully lift the basin from the water. Leave it to stand for 5 minutes. Take the sauce that you set aside earlier and heat it in a small pan until bubbling – keep stirring it so it doesn't stick and burn. Strain it through a small sieve into a warmed jug.

Take great care when taking the pudding out of the pan and removing the covers. The bowl will be scalding hot!

Cut the string, foil and paper off the basin. Loosen the sides of the pudding with a blunt-ended knife and turn the pudding out onto a deep plate. What a sight! Serve in generous wedges with hot gravy for pouring.

CRUMPETS

**Home-made crumpets are a million miles away from the rubbery packet versions.
They're as easy to make as they look, so make a big batch and toast as required.**

MAKES 12

350ml whole milk
225g strong white flour
125g plain flour
7g sachet fast-action dried yeast
½ tsp fine sea salt
1 tsp caster sugar
1 level tsp bicarbonate of soda
150ml warm water
softened butter, for greasing the rings

Put the milk in a saucepan and warm it very gently until tepid. Sift the flours into a large bowl and stir in the yeast, salt and sugar. Make a well in the centre and stir in the warm milk. Beat well with a wooden spoon for 3–4 minutes until the batter is thick and elastic. Cover with clingfilm and leave to rise in a warm place for an hour or until doubled in size.

Mix the bicarbonate of soda with the warm water. Beat this into the batter for a couple of minutes and leave to rest in a warm place for a further 30 minutes. By this time, the batter should look risen and be covered with tiny bubbles. Heat a flat griddle pan or large heavy-based non-stick frying pan over a medium-high heat.

Generously butter the insides of 4 crumpet rings or 9cm chef's rings and place them on the griddle or in the frying pan. Warm for a minute or two. Using a dessertspoon, drop 3 large spoonfuls of the crumpet batter into each ring. It should come about 1.5cm up the sides of each ring, but no more. Cook for 9–12 minutes or until lots of tiny bubbles have risen to the surface and burst and the tops look dry and set. Carefully lift off the rings – this shouldn't be too difficult as the crumpets will ease back from the sides when they are ready. (Use an oven cloth and take care as they will be hot.)

Flip the crumpets over with a spatula and cook on the other side for 2 minutes or until golden brown. You can keep these crumpets warm while the remaining batter is prepared, or serve immediately spread with lots of butter. Cook the rest of the crumpets in exactly the same way as the first, washing and buttering the rings well before using each time. (The crumpets can also be cooled and then toasted.)

When you make the last few crumpets, you may find that the batter has thickened and the bubbles take longer to burst. If this happens, prick each one lightly with a cocktail stick.

LEMON DRIZZLE CAKE

This is dead easy to make and really tasty. It's the one cake that the soggier it is, the better.

SERVES 10

2 small unwaxed lemons, well scrubbed
275g granulated sugar
175g unsalted butter, softened, plus
extra for greasing the tin
200g self-raising flour
½ tsp baking powder
3 large free-range eggs

Preheat the oven to 180°C/Gas 4. Line the base of a 900g (2lb) non-stick loaf tin with baking parchment and butter the tin well. Finely grate the zest of the lemons. Put 175g of the sugar in a food processor with the butter, flour, baking powder, eggs and lemon zest and blend on the pulse setting until the mixture is just combined and has a thick, smooth texture.

Spoon the cake batter into the prepared tin and level the surface. Bake for 35 minutes or until well risen and pale golden brown. Remove from the oven and cool in the tin for 5 minutes. Squeeze one of the lemons to get about 3 tablespoons of juice and mix this with the remaining 100g of granulated sugar.

Turn the cake out onto a wire rack set above a tray or plate. Remove the baking parchment and gently turn the cake the right way up. Make about 50 deep holes in the top of the cake with a skewer.

Slowly and gradually, spoon over half the lemon sugar, allowing it to thoroughly coat the top of the cake and drizzle down the sides. Leave the cake to stand for 5 minutes, then do the same with the remaining lemon sugar. Leave to set for at least an hour or until the sugar and lemon has crystallised. Serve the cake in thick slices with a nice cup of tea.

BUTTERFLY CAKES

Aida Grier and her daughter Victoria are amazingly talented bakers. We visited them
at their home in Perthshire and they put on an incredible spread for us. They're both
passionate about cooking and everything was really scrumptious – we had the best time.
Their recipes are brilliant, and things like the empire biscuits are dead easy for kids to make.

MAKES 12

110g baking margarine
110g caster sugar
110g beaten egg
110g self-raising flour

TOPPING
110g butter, room temperature
110g icing sugar, plus extra for dusting
grated zest of 1 orange
1 jar of orange curd

You will need a 12-hole bun tin, lined with paper cake cases.
Preheat the oven to 190°C/Gas 5.

Cream the margarine and sugar until light in colour, then
gradually add the beaten egg. Gently fold in the flour. Spoon
the mixture into the cake cases and bake for 12–15 minutes.
Turn the cakes out onto a wire rack and leave them to cool.

Cut the top off each cake and set aside. To make the butter
icing, mix the butter with the icing sugar and zest. Put half a
teaspoon of orange curd on each cake and top with a teaspoon
of butter icing. Cut the tops in half to make butterfly wing
shapes and add them to each cake. Dust with icing sugar.
For birthdays and parties, sprinkle with a little edible glitter.

You can use lemon curd instead of orange and add lemon zest
to the butter icing.

MRS MILLER'S EMPIRE BISCUITS

Mrs Miller is a lifelong friend of Aida's and a baking inspiration. Her cakes are legendary in the area.

MAKES 12

170g plain flour, plus extra for
sprinkling the baking tray
170g butter, room temperature
55g icing sugar
55g cornflour
1 pot of seedless raspberry jam
icing (optional)
glacé cherries (optional)

Preheat the oven to 190°C/Gas 5. Sprinkle a large baking tray
with flour. Mix all the ingredients together with your hands
until the mixture forms a soft dough. Roll it out to about 1cm
thick and cut into circles with a scone cutter. Place the biscuits
on the baking tray and bake for 10–12 minutes. The secret of
getting these biscuits perfect is to watch them carefully while
they are in the oven and remove them as soon as they are firm
to the touch but still pale. Leave them to cool on a wire rack.

When they are cool, sandwich the biscuits together with
raspberry jam and top with icing and a cherry if you like.

BRAN LOAF

Aida says that this works equally well with oat or wheat bran. The fat content
can be lessened by using low-fat milk, making it a great low-cholesterol treat.

MAKES 1 LOAF

1 mug of bran
1 mug of soft brown sugar
1 mug of sultanas or other dried fruit
1 mug of full-fat milk
1 mug of self-raising flour

Mix the bran, sugar, sultanas and milk together in a bowl
with a wooden spoon and leave to soak overnight. The next
day, grease and line a small (450g) loaf tin and preheat the
oven to 180°C/Gas 4. Stir the flour into the bran mixture, then
place the dough in the loaf tin and bake for 45–50 minutes
until firm to the touch. This loaf keeps well in a tin for a week
to 10 days, ideal if baking for one!

ROCKY ROAD

This is so easy to make and tastes wonderful. Aida says she uses large fluffy
marshmallows and leaves them whole – more of a boulder road really!

3 Mars bars
100g butter
5 shortbread fingers
140g marshmallows
50g Rice Krispies

Chop up the Mars bars and place them in a small pan with
the butter. Melt over a gentle heat. Break the shortbread
into chunks and stir into the mixture with the marshmallows
and Rice Krispies. Press the mixture into a lightly oiled
15cm-square tin and leave to set in the fridge. When set,
cut into squares, turn them out upside down and serve.

MILLIONAIRE'S SHORTBREAD

This is a truly decadent treat so don't skimp on the chocolate. Enjoy!

BASE
125g butter, room temperature
50g caster sugar
175g plain flour

Mix the butter, sugar and flour to form a dough. Press this into
a greased 23cm-square cake tin and bake at 190°C/Gas 5 for
20 minutes. Leave to cool.

TOPPING
400g condensed milk
50g butter
50g soft brown sugar
150g of your favourite chocolate

Meanwhile, make the topping. Pour the milk into a heavy-
bottomed pan and add the butter and sugar. Bring to the boil
and then boil gently for 5 minutes, stirring continuously so the
mixture doesn't stick. Pour the topping over the shortbread
and place in the fridge to set. Once the topping has set, melt
the chocolate in a bowl over a pan of simmering water and pour
it over the topping. Leave to set again and cut into squares.

FOUGASSE À L'ANCHOIS

François Gandolfi, one of our directors, gave us this recipe. This is what he told us about it:
'This is a version of a popular Provençal snack called anchoïade, which is a paste made of anchovies, onion or garlic and olive oil into which you dip raw vegetables. Then someone decided that the paste would be nice spread on bread and to make this more child-friendly my mum transformed it into a kind of garlic bread with a twist. Rachel, my wife, loves it but she has changed the recipe a little. Here are both versions – frankly, I prefer my wife's, but don't tell my mum! The dough is the same in both – it's a traditional focaccia dough, but you can use a pizza-type dough instead. For both recipes, use anchovies in olive oil rather than those in salt or brine.'

SERVES 6

DOUGH
2 tbsp olive oil
450g strong white flour
1 tsp salt
7g dried yeast
275ml water

MUM'S ANCHOÏADE
12 anchovies in oil
1 onion, peeled and roughly chopped
4 tbsp olive oil

RACHEL'S ANCHOÏADE
1 x 60g jar of anchovies in oil
2 large garlic cloves, peeled
10 green olives
2 tbsp olive oil
(use the oil from the jar of anchovies)

Mix all the dough ingredients in a large bowl to make a smooth but sticky dough. Leave it to rise for 30 minutes and knead again for about 10 minutes. Alternatively, put everything in a bread machine and let that do the work for you!

Roll the dough out into 2 large ovals and cut several slashes in each one with a knife – these make it easier to tear the fougasse apart. Leave the dough to rest again for at least 45 minutes while you make the anchoïade. Preheat the oven to 200°/Gas 6.

For mum's anchoïade, use a pestle and mortar to mash all the ingredients into a paste. For Rachel's recipe, use a hand-held blender to mix everything into a smooth paste. Spread the paste over the dough. It will be a thin layer, but the taste is strong so you don't need much. Place the fougasse on a baking tray and bake for 15–20 minutes – take care that they don't dry out too much.

Drizzle a little olive oil on top and enjoy with a glass of cold rosé wine. Best eaten as a snack with drinks or with a simple soup, as the strong anchovy flavour overpowers most other tastes.

CHEESE NIBBLES

Duncan Barnes, our other director, sent us this recipe and the one below from his mum. She describes them as simple but great to nibble with coffee and a chat, and says she must have made thousands over the years.

MAKES ABOUT 30

170g self-raising flour
110g soft margarine
½ tsp mustard or horseradish (optional)
170g strong cheese, such as mature Cheddar, grated

Preheat the oven to 190°C/Gas 5. Put the flour, margarine and mustard or horseradish (if using) into a bowl and mix until it has the texture of breadcrumbs. Add the cheese and mix again with your hands.

Take a large teaspoon of the mixture, make it into a little ball with your fingers and place on a large baking tray. Continue until all the mixture is used up, taking care to leave space between each one. Bake in the oven for 10–12 minutes until golden. Remove from the oven and immediately take the nibbles off the baking tray with a fish slice or palette knife or they will stick. Place them on a wire rack and eat warm or cold. If you like, you can put an olive, date or peanut into each one before baking as a little surprise for the eater.

COFFEE KISSES

Tasty nuggets of coffee cookies – just right with a cup of tea in the afternoon.

MAKES ABOUT 24

170g self-raising flour
85g butter or margarine
55g white sugar
1 egg yolk or very small whole egg
1 large tsp liquid coffee (or dissolve
1 tsp instant coffee in boiling water)

In a large bowl, mix the flour, butter and sugar until the mixture has a breadcrumb-like texture. Add the egg and coffee and mix again to make a firm dough.

Preheat the oven to 190°C/Gas 5. Take teaspoons of the mixture and roll into small balls with your hands. Place the balls on a baking sheet, leaving space between each one as they will spread, and bake for 15 minutes. Remove and place on a wire rack to cool.

ICING
55g very soft butter
120g icing sugar, more if needed
few drops of vanilla essence
icing sugar (optional)

Meanwhile, make the butter icing. Put the soft butter in a bowl and beat in enough icing sugar to make a thick butter cream icing. Add the vanilla essence. When the cookies are cold, spread half of them with butter cream and top with the rest to make sandwiches. Dust with icing sugar if you like.

WOMEN'S INSTITUTE

The WI movement began in Canada in 1897. The first British Women's Institute was formed in 1915 with two main aims: to provide education and to improve the quality of rural life, and it led to women playing a major part in the First World War. Since then, the aims have broadened and it is now the largest women's organisation in the UK. In 2005, the British WI celebrated its 90th anniversary and there are currently 205,000 members in 6,500 WIs. Members from the North Yorkshire West Federation visited the Mums Know Best recipe fair and provided these recipes.

LEMON, GINGER & BLUEBERRY FLAN

This simple but delicious pudding takes a while to set, so make it the night before serving if possible.

SERVES 6–8

150g ginger biscuits
50g butter, melted
500ml double cream
150g caster sugar
juice and grated zest of 2 lemons
150g blueberries
fresh mint leaves and icing sugar for garnish

Put the ginger biscuits in a plastic bag and crush them into crumbs with a rolling pin. Add the melted butter, mix well and use the mixture to line a loose-bottomed 20cm flan tin. Press it down firmly. Pour the cream into a small saucepan and add the sugar and the lemon zest. Bring to the boil and continue to boil for 3–4 minutes, watching carefully.

Remove from the heat and stir in the lemon juice. Strain the mixture through a fine sieve to remove the lemon zest and leave to cool for a few minutes. Spread the blueberries over the prepared flan base, reserving some for decoration, and pour in the cream mixture. Allow to set in the fridge. Before serving, decorate the top with blueberries, mint leaves and a dusting of icing sugar.

A NEW LOOK
AT SCONES

If the WI doesn't know how to make a good scone, no one does. Here's a great
recipe for the perfect tea time treat – the yoghurt helps the scones to rise.

MAKES 12–14

340g self-raising flour
pinch of salt
85g butter, plus extra for greasing
55g caster sugar
125ml milk
4 tbsp natural yoghurt

Preheat the oven to 220°C/Gas 7 and lightly grease a baking
sheet. Sift together the flour and salt into a bowl and rub
in the butter until the mixture resembles fine breadcrumbs.
Stir in the sugar and add the milk and yoghurt. Work the
mixture together until a soft dough is formed.

Turn the dough out onto a floured surface and knead lightly,
then flatten it out to an even thickness of about 2cm. Using a
5cm cutter, cut out the scones and place them on the baking
tray. Gather the trimmings and cut out more scones.

Bake for 12–15 minutes until brown. Remove the scones from
the oven and leave them to cool on a wire rack.

To make savoury scones, replace the caster sugar with 55g
of grated Cheddar cheese and half a teaspoon of mustard
powder. Prepare and bake the scones in the same way.

Show-off food

CHICKEN IN BRANDY

Muriel Bell is a lovely lady who lives in Tenbury Wells in Worcestershire. Her mum
was in service in a big house and Muriel still has her book of recipes, all hand-written.
Muriel's chicken is a super-rich treat – good for entertaining and a real show-off dish.

SERVES 6

splash of olive oil
30g butter
6 chicken breasts
1 red onion, finely diced
100ml good brandy
170g white button mushrooms, wiped
and trimmed
100ml double cream
sea salt and black pepper

Preheat the oven to 150°C/Gas 2. Heat the olive oil and butter
in a large frying pan. Add the chicken breasts and cook briefly
to seal in the juices. Add the diced onion and cook until
translucent but not coloured.

Remove the pan from the heat. Warm the brandy, pour it into
the pan and ignite, then wait for the flames to die down. Add
the mushrooms, pour over the cream and season well.

Transfer everything to an ovenproof dish and cover with foil.
Bake in the preheated oven for about an hour. Serve with some
rich mustard mash.

MUSTARD MASH

SERVES 6

1kg potatoes, peeled and quartered
75ml single cream
50g butter
2 tbsp grain mustard
sea salt and black pepper

Put the potatoes into a pan of salted water, bring to the boil
and poach them for about 20 minutes until soft – poaching
the potatoes rather than boiling them makes a fluffier mash.
Warm the cream in a separate pan.

When the potatoes are cooked, drain them well and return
them to the pan to drive off any excess moisture, then mash.
Add the warm cream, butter and mustard and mix well.
Season to taste.

LEMON SOUFFLÉ

This is one of Muriel's mum's recipes. Princess Margaret used to visit the house where she worked and this was one of the princess's favourite dishes, which she'd ask to be made specially. In fact, this is not really a soufflé, despite the name. It's a set pudding and more like a mousse.

SERVES 4–6

14g sachet of gelatine
2 medium eggs, separated
200g caster sugar
juice and grated zest of 2 large lemons
300ml double cream, plus extra
for garnish
100g hazelnuts or mixed nuts,
chopped
100g green grapes, halved

Lightly grease a soufflé dish. Take a piece of greaseproof paper and tie it around the dish to make a collar standing about 5cm above the rim. Make sure it's tied really tightly.

To prepare the gelatine, pour 4 tablespoons of very hot water into a bowl and sprinkle in the gelatine. Place the bowl over a pan of hot water until the gelatine has dissolved. Leave to cool slightly.

Whisk the egg yolks and sugar together until thick and creamy and add the lemon zest and juice. Pour in the cooled gelatine mixture and mix gently but thoroughly.

Whisk the cream to the 'floppy' stage. In a separate bowl, whisk the egg whites until they form stiff peaks. Fold the cream into the yolk and gelatine mixture, then fold in the egg whites.

Pour the mixture into the soufflé dish – it should fill to above the rim but be held by the greaseproof collar. Leave the pudding to set in the fridge for about 2 hours. When ready to serve, remove the collar and decorate with chopped nuts, gently pressing them onto the sides above the dish. Finish the top with whipped cream and halved grapes.

For an extra-special touch, add some crystallised lemon zest as shown in the picture opposite. Remove some fine strips of lemon zest with a zester and blanch them briefly in boiling water. Drain well and leave to dry. Put them in a bowl with a few tablespoons of caster sugar and toss well. Leave overnight.

PROPER PRAWN COCKTAIL

This is a culinary old faithful and an absolute must as a starter in the King household on Christmas Day. Make your own mayonnaise, get great seafood and tuck in. Use whatever sort of prawns you like, even frozen ones, in individual cocktails or make one big posh lobster cocktail (as pictured opposite) for a really spectacular effect. It might all look a bit camp, but it tastes wonderful.

SERVES 4

500g prawns
4 tbsp home-made mayonnaise
2 tsp tomato ketchup
1 tsp tomato purée
dash of Tabasco sauce
1 tsp salad cream
1 tsp lemon juice
4 little gem lettuces, shredded
75g tom berries or cherry tomatoes
lemon slices
paprika to garnish

If the prawns are raw, simply cook them in boiling water for a minute or two until they are cooked through. Set them aside to cool. Shell the prawns, but keep some whole ones to garnish the cocktails. In a bowl, mix the mayonnaise, ketchup, tomato purée, Tabasco sauce, salad cream and lemon juice. Mix the shredded lettuce with the tom berries or halved cherry tomatoes.

Fill each sundae glass two-thirds full with salad. Mix the prawns with the sauce and spoon onto the salad. Garnish with a whole prawn hanging over the edge of the glass with a slice of lemon for company and add a sprinkling of paprika. To make one big cocktail, prepare everything in the same way, but use some lobster meat and garnish with a whole lobster or two!

FOOLPROOF MAYONNAISE

We use a food processor for this, but you can make it almost as easily with a whisk or fork.

SERVES 4

2 egg yolks
1 whole egg
1 tbsp French mustard
juice of ½ lemon
½ tsp salt
½ tsp black pepper
½ tsp caster sugar
400ml vegetable oil

Place everything, except the oil, in a food processor. Blitz for 10 seconds to combine, then drizzle in the oil. When the oil is all in, blitz for another 10 seconds and there you have it – perfect mayonnaise. You'll never buy another jar again.

You can play around with this recipe and add lemon or lime zest for a citrus mayo or garlic to make a garlic mayo as strong or subtle as you like.

SÜLT

Eele Prints-De Tisi gave us this recipe. Eele is from Estonia, but is married to an Englishman and now lives in Bristol. She loves to cook traditional Estonian dishes and this jellied meat dish is one of her favourites. Unlike brawn, which can be a bit of mystery, it's clear what's in this and it looks great. You can use any herbs you like and make the sült in one big mould or a number of smaller ones.

SERVES 10–12

2 pig's trotters, chopped in half
1 pork hock
6–7 tbsp salt
2 tsp black peppercorns
2 bay leaves
1–2 tsp ground black pepper
1 tbsp gelatine (optional)
1 carrot, peeled and cooked

Wash the trotters and hock and put them in a stock pot. Cover with plenty of cold water and add a generous tablespoon of salt. Bring to the boil and boil rapidly for 5 minutes. Pour the water away, wash the meat and rinse the pot. Return the meat to the pot.

Now, add just enough cold water to cover the meat. Add the peppercorns, bay leaves and 2 generous tablespoons of salt. Boil over a low heat for 2–3 hours, until the meat is falling off the bones – it's important to keep the water boiling gently, otherwise the jelly will form a haze.

When the meat is cooked, lift it out and set it aside to cool slightly. Pour the liquid through a fine sieve to remove any small pieces of bone and take out any particles from the pot. Pour the liquid back into the pot and keep it warm.

Remove all the meat from the bones and dice into 1cm cubes. Add these to the liquid. Add the ground pepper and 3–4 tablespoons of salt. It's important to make the liquid taste strong – too salty – because the taste weakens as the dish cools. Bring everything to the boil and if you are not sure the jelly will set, add some gelatine.

Slice the carrot and cut it into decorative shapes. Place a piece of carrot at the bottom of each mould and ladle hot meat and liquid on top. Set aside to cool and put into the fridge when cold. To serve, ease the sült out of the mould and serve with hot boiled potatoes with vinegar, mustard or horseradish sauce.

KRINGEL

Every Estonian family has a recipe for kringel and this is Eele's version. It's a pretzel-shaped yeast bread with raisins and chocolate sauce and makes a great party cake. We tried a savoury version with grated cheese, too.

MAKES 1 LOAF

DOUGH
40g fresh yeast
1 tbsp sugar
250ml milk, lukewarm
2 egg yolks
400g plain flour
50g butter, melted

FILLING
100g butter, softened
3 handfuls of raisins
10 tsp sugar

TOPPING
150g dark chocolate
(at least 50% cocoa solids)
75g butter

Mix the yeast and sugar in a bowl. Add the lukewarm milk and egg yolks, then mix in the flour and melted butter and knead well. Shape the dough into a ball, cover the bowl with a kitchen towel and leave to rise in a warm place for 30 minutes.

Preheat the oven to 200°C/Gas 6. Dust your work surface with flour. Take the dough out of the bowl, knock it back and roll out to a thickness of about 1cm. Spread the soft butter evenly over the rolled sheet of pastry, then sprinkle with raisins and finally sugar.

Roll the dough up like a Swiss roll and cut it in half with a sharp knife. Starting from the uncut end, plait the dough, lifting each half over the other in turn. Finally, shape the plaited bread into a B-shape and transfer to a buttered baking tray. Bake for about 25 minutes or until golden.

In the meantime, prepare the chocolate topping by melting the chocolate and butter in a bowl over some boiling water. Once out of the oven, let the bread cool down a bit, place on a serving plate and drizzle on the chocolate sauce.

CHEESE KRINGEL
To make this savoury version, leave out the raisins and sugar and sprinkle the kringel with grated cheddar instead. Add more grated cheese on top instead of chocolate sauce.

ROOSA-MANNA

This is one of Eele's favourite recipes from her childhood – it was made by her grandma, her mum and now by her. It's a way of making semolina attractive by infusing it with fruit juice and a little bit of magic happens when the milk is poured on.

SERVES 4

300ml redcurrant juice
150g sugar
75g semolina
redcurrants for garnish (optional)

Pour the juice into a saucepan and add 300ml of water and the sugar. The mixture should taste strongly of both juice and sugar as the whipping will dilute the flavour.

Bring the liquid to boil. Sprinkle in the semolina while stirring continuously. The semolina cooks quickly and should take just a few minutes.

Once ready, cool the mixture for 5–10 minutes by placing the pan in a sink filled with cold water. Whip with a hand whisk until light and fluffy and pour straight into dessert bowls or glasses. Serve with cold milk poured over the top and garnish with some redcurrants if you like.

WHOLE POACHED SALMON

As seen at wedding receptions, christenings and so on all round the country, a beautifully decorated poached salmon, complete with cucumber scales, makes a perfect centrepiece. It looks impressive but it's simple to make and just takes patience and care. Follow our method below to get perfectly cooked salmon every time.

SERVES 8–10

1 x 2–3kg salmon, gutted and scaled
1 lemon, halved
1 dsrtsp black peppercorns
2 bay leaves
2 cucumbers
mayonnaise (see page 57)
fresh herbs and extra lemon slices
for garnish

Place the salmon in a large roasting tin or fish kettle and cover with cold water. Squeeze the juice from the lemon halves into the water and chuck in the rinds. Add the peppercorns and bay leaves.

Place the pan on the stove and bring to the boil. As soon as the water has boiled, remove the pan from the heat and leave the salmon to cool in the liquid. This way, the salmon will be perfectly cooked and still juicy. Be warned – there is nothing worse than dry poached salmon. Better to be underdone than cremated.

Remove the fish very carefully and place it on your presentation platter. Starting from just behind the gills, remove the skin from the presentation side. Now prepare to enjoy yourself. Cut the cucumbers into thin slices and, with the artistry of Rolf Harris, apply them to the salmon to look like scales. Pipe mayonnaise on and around the salmon as you like and garnish with herbs.

Gorgeous.

CORONATION CHICKEN

This dish became famous when it was served at the coronation luncheon of Elizabeth II in 1953. It's been through many variations – Dave's mam used to make it with a handful of sultanas, mayonnaise, a teaspoon of mild curry powder and some cold roast chicken. This is our modern version, which is fit for the best of occasions.

SERVES 4

2 free-range chicken breasts, boned and skinned
1 tbsp olive oil
zest of 1 lemon, finely chopped
knob of butter
1 shallot, finely chopped
1 red chilli, seeded and finely chopped
2 tsp Madras curry powder
2 tbsp tomato paste
100ml dry white wine
1 tbsp apricot jam
100ml chicken stock
150ml mayonnaise (see page 57)
75ml crème fraîche
1 large mango, peeled and diced
4 spring onions, trimmed and finely chopped
juice of 1 lemon
2 tbsp chopped fresh coriander
dash of Tabasco sauce
sea salt flakes and ground black pepper to taste
green salad to serve
50g flaked almonds (optional)

First rub the chicken with olive oil. Scatter on the lemon zest and season with salt and black pepper. Place the chicken in a steamer – the Chinese bamboo ones work well for this – and steam for about 20 minutes or until the chicken is cooked through. Set aside to cool. The chicken will be fragrant and juicy.

Melt the butter in a frying pan, add the shallot and chilli and sweat gently for about 5 minutes. Stir in the curry powder and cook for a few minutes more, then stir in the tomato paste and cook for a further minute. Add the wine and cook hard until the liquid is reduced by half. Add the jam and stock, then continue to simmer until again reduced by half. Set this mixture aside to cool.

Mix the mayonnaise and crème fraîche in a bowl. Stir in the cooled curry mixture, then add the mango, spring onions, lemon juice and coriander. Fold in the chicken, cut into bite-sized pieces, then add Tabasco and seasoning to taste. Serve with green salad. You can also toast some flaked almonds in a dry frying pan and scatter these over the chicken just before serving if you wish.

BAKED ALASKA

Tessa Johnstone gave us this recipe. She lives in Chippenham, Wiltshire, and has loved cooking since she was a child. Her dad was a yacht designer and her mum used to host dinner parties to entertain clients. Baked Alaska was her dad's party piece – he would finish it off by browning the meringue with a blowtorch at the table. This certainly provides the proper wow factor – but watch the curtains.

SERVES 6

225g fresh raspberries
2 tbsp Cointreau
or similar orange liqueur
20cm sponge flan base
4 egg whites
170g caster sugar
1 litre good vanilla ice cream

Put the raspberries in a bowl and pour on the Cointreau. Leave to macerate for 2 hours.

Preheat the oven to 230°C/Gas 8. Place the sponge base on a baking tray and spoon on most of the soaked raspberries and juice.

Whisk the egg whites until stiff and then gradually whisk in the sugar. Fill a piping bag with this meringue mix.

Scoop the ice cream onto the raspberries and add the rest of the raspberries on top. Immediately pipe the meringue over and around the ice cream – no gaps! Put the Alaska straight into the preheated oven for about 4 minutes until browned.

Serve at once – it won't wait.

Instead of browning the meringue in the oven, you can use a blowtorch like Tessa's dad used to do. Take great care, though, and as soon as a patch of meringue turns golden, move the torch to the next bit or it will burn.

HONEY & MARMALADE ROASTED GAMMON

This is a fusion of tips from both our mams. Si's mam says, 'Using half orange juice and half water to simmer the ham makes it sweet and tasty.' Dave's mam says, 'Use marmalade for a lovely sticky glaze.' We serve it with an apple compote and pickled red cabbage and it's great for a buffet.

SERVES 20 PLUS

1 x 6kg gammon joint
fresh orange juice
2 onions
lots of cloves
4 large bay leaves

GLAZE

120g soft brown sugar
zest of 3 oranges
juice of 1 orange
3 tbsp runny honey
3 heaped tbsp orange marmalade
3 tbsp wholegrain mustard

Place the gammon joint in a large saucepan. Cover with water, bring to the boil and discard the water. This gets rid of any excess salt in the gammon very quickly – a top tip.

Pour the orange juice into the pan until it reaches halfway up the gammon and top up with cold water to cover. Cut the onions in half and put 2 cloves in each half. Add the onions to the pan with the bay leaves, then cover and simmer for about 3 hours. Keep an eye on the level of liquid and top up with boiling water as needed.

At the end of the cooking time, remove the gammon from the saucepan and place it in a roasting tin. Remove the skin, but leave a good layer of fat. Using a sharp knife, score the surface of the gammon into diamond shapes. Stud the centre of each diamond with a clove.

Then make the glaze. Mix together the soft brown sugar, orange zest and juice, honey, marmalade and mustard.

Preheat the oven to 180°C/Gas 4. Spoon the glaze over the gammon, place it in the preheated oven and roast for 45 minutes, basting frequently.

Eat the gammon hot in thin slices with mash and juice or serve it cold. Delicious either way.

QUICK DILL PICKLED CABBAGE

Simple to make and a perfect sweet and sour accompaniment to the gammon.

SERVES 6

1 red cabbage
250ml white wine vinegar
100g granulated sugar
4 tsp salt
handful of fresh dill, chopped

Remove the outer leaves of the cabbage and the core and slice the rest finely.

Pour the vinegar into a saucepan and add the sugar, salt and 125ml of water. Bring to the boil, then add the cabbage and stir well. Remove from the heat, cover and leave to cool for an hour. Add the chopped dill and leave to infuse for another hour before serving.

APPLE COMPOTE

Some sort of apple sauce is a must with any kind of pork and this is a good one.

SERVES 6

150g caster sugar
½ tsp ground cinnamon
6 cloves
500g cooking apples

Put the sugar in a saucepan and add 500ml of water. Heat until a syrup forms and add the cinnamon and cloves.

Peel the apples, core them and cut into quarters. Add them to the syrup and simmer until soft. Smash the apples up a bit and serve with the gammon. Keep some to have cold with the ham sarnies, too.

LILL'S PRETZELS

Lill, Dave's missus, is from Romania. During Ceausescu's reign, her father worked in a factory and while he was there he made a metal pretzel cutter for his daughter. When Lill first came to England she had very little, but she did bring her special pretzel cutter, made by her dad with a lot of love. If you don't have one, just use an ordinary biscuit cutter to stamp out the pretzels.

MAKES ABOUT 30

2 eggs
350g plain flour
250g Cheddar cheese, grated, plus extra for the topping
250g butter, margarine, or lard
2 tbsp caraway seeds
pinch of salt

Beat one of the eggs in a bowl and add the flour, cheese, butter, 1 tablespoon of the caraway seeds and a pinch of salt. Mix well to make a dough, then leave to rest for an hour.

Preheat the oven to 180°C/Gas 4. Roll out the dough to a thickness of about 1cm and cut out the pretzels. Place them on a greased baking tray. Beat the other egg and use it to brush the pretzels, then sprinkle with the rest of the caraway seeds and some grated cheese. Bake for 10–15 minutes or until golden. Remove and cool on a wire rack.

WEST AFRICAN GHANAIAN COMMUNITY GROUP

The centre of this community group is The Gold Coast, a family restaurant in south London. The restaurant opened in 2004 and is run by William and Francesca Quagraine, both from Ghana, who were inspired by their love of food and the rich culture of their homeland. The Gold Coast has now become a focal point for the Ghanaian community in London and specialises in cooking West African recipes passed down through generations.

GUINEA FOWL WITH RED CHILLI
(AKONFEM)

Guinea fowl can be cooked just like chicken but it has a delicious, slightly gamey flavour. The birds are native to West Africa and feature in many Ghanaian dishes.

SERVES 2

1 x 1.5–2kg guinea fowl without giblets

MARINADE
1 garlic clove
25g root ginger, peeled
½ medium white onion, peeled and chopped
100ml vegetable oil
1 tbsp dried crushed red chillies

To prepare the marinade, place the garlic, fresh ginger, white onion and vegetable oil in a blender. Blend until smooth and thick and then mix in the dried crushed red chillies.

Cut the guinea fowl from the breast down to the stomach and open it out like a book. Brush the guinea fowl with the marinade inside and out and place it flat in an oven dish. Pour any excess marinade on top of the guinea fowl to ensure it is well covered and leave it in the fridge for 2 hours.

Preheat the oven to 180°C/Gas 4. Bake the guinea fowl in its marinade on the middle shelf of the oven for 30 minutes. Take care not to overcook it – you want the meat to stay juicy. Alternatively, barbecue the guinea fowl for about 30 minutes, turning it regularly. Serve with vegetables and yam balls.

YAM BALLS

An ideal accompaniment to the guinea fowl opposite as part of a splendid Ghanaian feast.
Puna or white yams are the most popular variety in Ghana.

SERVES 5 AS AN APPETIZER

1kg puna yams
½ red pepper
½ green pepper
½ yellow pepper
1 spring onion
3 tbsp margarine
2 egg yolks
4 egg whites
breadcrumbs
500ml vegetable oil, for deep frying

Boil the puna yams until cooked through and soft to the touch. Drain, place in a bowl and mash until they form a smooth paste. Finely chop all the peppers and the spring onion and dry them on kitchen paper, squeezing out any excess water. Stir them into the puna yam mash and add the margarine and egg yolks. Mix well.

Place the egg whites in a bowl and the breadcrumbs in a separate bowl. Mould the puna yam mash mixture into small balls, about the size of golf balls.

Dip the balls into the egg white, then the breadcrumbs and repeat this process twice for each ball. Half fill a deep saucepan with oil or use a deep-fat fryer. Heat the oil to 100–120°C and fry the yam balls until golden brown.

Good
simple
suppers

MEAT & POTATO PIE

Fiona Armitage lives in Ilkley, West Yorkshire and we met her with her mum, Sybil.
Although Fiona doesn't do that much cooking herself she does love good food and has become
more interested since finding a book of her great-aunt's handwritten recipes. These include
many from Fiona's grandmother and other members of the family. Fiona made us this pie from her
granny's recipe, but her mum made the pastry, which was top-notch – every northerner's dream.
Sybil got a special gold star from us. You need to start this pie the day before by making the stock.

STOCK
couple of marrow bones
4 carrots, roughly chopped
2 celery sticks, roughly chopped
2 bay leaves
4 peppercorns
500g beef shin, roughly chopped

PIE
1kg stewing steak
1 tbsp vegetable oil
2 onions, peeled and chopped
2 carrots, peeled and chopped
2 celery sticks, chopped
500g potatoes, peeled and chopped
shortcrust pastry (see page 14)
1 egg, beaten
sea salt and black pepper to taste

First make the stock. Roast the marrow bones in the oven
at 180°C/Gas 4 for 45–60 minutes or until well browned.
Transfer the roasted bones to a large pot and add the remaining
ingredients. Pour in enough cold water to cover, bring to the
boil and simmer gently for 4–5 hours. Keep an eye on the
pan and top up with boiling water when necessary.

At the end of the cooking time, remove the bones and boil
the liquid until reduced by half. Leave to cool, then skim off
the fat. Liquidise the vegetables.

Now the pie. Preheat the oven to 150°C/Gas 2. Cut the
stewing steak into cubes, roughly 2.5cm square. Heat the oil
in a frying pan and brown the meat, then transfer it to a large
ovenproof pot. Add the onions, carrots and celery to the frying
pan and sweat them gently until soft. Add them to the meat
and pour in the stock to cover. Season to taste. Cook in the
oven for 3 hours, then add the potatoes and cook for another
hour. Remove and leave to cool.

Turn the oven up to 180°C/Gas 4. Pile the filling into a 1.2 litre
pie dish and brush the edges of the dish with beaten egg. Roll
out the pastry on a well-floured board and place it gently over
the filling. Press the edges firmly to seal and trim neatly. Flute
the edges or leave them plain, as you prefer. Decorate the top
with any excess pastry and brush with beaten egg to glaze.
Place the dish on a baking sheet and bake in the centre of
the oven for about 30 minutes until golden on top.

PICCALILLI

This is a great piccalilli recipe from Fiona's great-aunt's recipe book. Fiona says that her great-aunt would have soaked and cooked dried kidney beans, but canned ones work just fine.

MAKES 3 JARS

½ vegetable marrow
½ cucumber
1 onion, peeled
225g canned kidney beans or cauliflower florets
salt
55g sugar
55g flour
1 tbsp English mustard powder
55g turmeric
1 tbsp ground ginger
1.2 litres white wine vinegar

Cut the vegetables into small pieces and put them on a plate with the beans (if using). Sprinkle everything with salt and leave overnight.

Mix the sugar, flour and spices to a paste with a spoonful of the vinegar. Pour the rest of the vinegar into a saucepan and bring to the boil. Add the paste and boil for 5 minutes. Take the pan off the heat and add the vegetables. Ladle the piccalilli into sterilised jars and cover with waxed discs and cellophane or lids.

TOMATO CHUTNEY

And here is Fiona's granny's classic tomato chutney recipe.

MAKES 3 SMALL JARS

450g tomatoes
110g sour apples
225g onions
110g sugar
1 tsp salt
1 tsp ground ginger
good pinch of cayenne pepper
300ml wine vinegar

Pour boiling water over the tomatoes, then slip off the skins. Cut them into slices. Peel and core the apples and chop them finely. Peel and chop the onions.

Put all the ingredients into a large saucepan and bring to the boil. Cook for up to an hour, stirring often, until the chutney has thickened. Pour into sterilised jars and leave to cool. Cover with waxed discs and cellophane or lids.

DAVE'S MAM'S KILLER FISHCAKES
WITH CHEDDAR CHEESE SAUCE

These are lovely, but they nearly were killer fishcakes. As three-year old Dave sat sucking the key to his clockwork monkey, he was distracted by the delicious smell of fishcakes cooking. One gulp and the key lodged in his throat – he had to have an operation to remove it! So no fishcakes for Dave for a while, but he did have lots of ice cream.

SERVES 6

500g hake steaks
250ml milk
1 bay leaf
3 eggs
1 heaped tbsp chopped curly parsley
500g cold buttery mashed potatoes
4 tbsp plain flour
1 packet of golden breadcrumbs –
the bright orange ones!
vegetable oil for shallow frying
black pepper and white pepper
sea salt

CHEDDAR CHEESE SAUCE
reserved fish stock
whole milk
50g unsalted butter
2 tbsp plain flour
175g Cheddar cheese, grated
salt and pepper

First, poach the hake. Preheat the oven to 150°C/Gas 2. Put the fish in an ovenproof dish, season with ground black pepper and sea salt, then pour in the milk. Add the bay leaf, cover the dish with foil and bake for about 25 minutes until the fish is just cooked and falls away from the bone. Leave to cool, then carefully flake the fish, removing all the bones, and set aside. Strain the milky fish stock and set it aside for making the cheese sauce.

Beat one of the eggs. Gently fold the fish, beaten egg and chopped parsley into the mashed potatoes. Season to taste with salt and pepper – use white pepper this time as it tastes better in mash for some reason.

Form the mixture into 4 large cakes. Beat the other 2 eggs in a bowl and pour the flour and some breadcrumbs onto separate plates. Roll the fishcakes in flour, dip in beaten egg, then roll in the luminous crumbs.

Heat the oil in a frying pan and fry these monsters gently until warmed through and golden.

TO MAKE THE CHEESE SAUCE
Make the fish stock up to 500ml by adding milk. Melt the butter in a pan, stir in the flour and cook for 3 minutes. Gradually whisk in the milky stock and cook gently until the sauce thickens. Add the cheese and stir it in until it melts. Season to taste and pour this cheesy duvet over a monolith of a fishcake.

SPICY ROASTED CHICKEN
WITH MINTY SAUCE

Harjinder Kaur lives in Manchester. She's a brilliant cook and we think she could make a curry out of anything. Harjinder learned how to cook from her mum and she told us that her knowledge of spicing dishes has been passed down through generations. Her use of spices is just right – everything she cooked was perfectly spiced and tasted great.

SERVES 4–6

1kg chicken thighs, skinned/washed and drained
4cm piece of root ginger, peeled and finely chopped
juice of ½ lemon
1½ tsp salt
1 tsp ground peppercorns and coriander seeds
1 tsp paprika
½ tsp garam masala (see page 90)
1½ tsp whole cumin seeds
oil, for greasing tin

MINTY YOGHURT SAUCE
500ml plain yoghurt
2 dsrtsp ready-made mint sauce

Wash and dry the chicken thighs and make 3 slits in each one with a sharp knife. Place the chicken in a bowl and add the ginger, lemon juice, salt and spices. Mix well and leave to marinate for 10 minutes.

Preheat the oven to 220°C/Gas 7. Oil a roasting tin and add the marinated chicken, spreading it out evenly, and roast for 45 minutes.

To make the minty yoghurt sauce, add the mint sauce to the yoghurt and mix them well. Serve the sauce chilled with the hot chicken.

CURRIED SALMON

Another great recipe from Harjinder and an excellent way of cheering up a bit of farmed salmon.

SERVES 6

1kg salmon steaks or salmon fillet, descaled
5 garlic cloves, finely chopped
4cm piece of root ginger, finely chopped
1 or 2 green chillies, deseeded and chopped (optional)
1 x 400g can of chopped tomatoes
2 fresh tomatoes, sliced
handful of fresh coriander, chopped

SPICE MIX

2½ tsp salt
1 tsp ground peppercorns and coriander seeds
1 tsp paprika
½ tsp garam masala
2 tsp cumin seeds
2 tsp lovage seeds
½ tsp dried red chilli flakes (add more or less according to taste)
2 tsp turmeric

TARKA MIX

3 tbsp vegetable oil
1 tsp lovage seeds
1 tsp cumin seeds
4 garlic cloves, finely chopped

Wash the salmon in salty water, rinse in fresh water and drain well. Cut the salmon into large chunks and place in a bowl. Add all the spice mix and gently toss the fish so it is covered with the spices. Add the chopped garlic, ginger and chillies if using and gently toss again to mix everything together. Set aside for 10 minutes.

Now prepare the tarka mix in which the salmon will be cooked. Heat the vegetable oil in a frying pan. Add the lovage seeds and fry them until they are almost black, then add the cumin seeds and fry for another 5 seconds. Add the 4 cloves of chopped garlic and fry until slightly golden, then add the salmon.

Cook on medium heat, moving the fish around by gently shaking the pan until the oil begins to separate from spices and the salmon is sealed and brown. Add about 225ml of hot water and the canned and fresh tomatoes, bring to the boil and simmer for a few minutes until the fish is cooked through. Sprinkle on the chopped coriander and remove from heat. Serve with boiled rice.

HARJINDER'S PAKORAS

The recipe below includes onion and potato, but Harjinder says you can use any vegetables you like, such as aubergines, cauliflower and broccoli. Most just need to be parboiled and cooled, but potatoes should be boiled in their skins until cooked, then sliced thickly. To prepare Harjinder's garam masala, grind equal amounts of cinnamon sticks, large cardamom pods and cloves until finely ground.

SERVES 6

450g gram (chick pea) flour
2 tsp baking powder
3 onions, peeled and thinly sliced
1 bunch of spring onions, chopped
5cm piece of root ginger, peeled and chopped
handful of fresh coriander, chopped
2 green chillies, deseeded and chopped
(optional)
350g potatoes, boiled in skins, sliced
vegetable oil for deep frying

SPICE MIX

1½ tsp salt
1½ tsp black peppercorns and coriander seeds
2 tsp cumin seeds and 2 tsp lovage seeds
1½ tsp paprika
½ tsp home-made garam masala (see above)

Mix the gram flour with the baking powder and spice mix in a bowl. Slowly add cold water, about 350ml, to make a batter with a dropping consistency.

Add the onions, spring onions, ginger, coriander and chillies, if using, and mix together really well. This is best done with your hands. Then mix in the potatoes, working gently so they don't break up too much.

Heat the oil to moderately hot in a large pan. Carefully put spoonfuls of the mixture into the oil – a few at a time. Cook gently for 7–8 minutes, turning the pakoras in the oil from time to time to make sure they cook evenly.

Drain and serve with mint chutney (below) as a starter or side dish or with rotis for a light lunch or supper.

MINT CHUTNEY

2 onions, peeled and quartered
2 green chillies, deseeded
3 tomatoes, halved
5cm piece of root ginger, peeled
handful of coriander
3 tbsp mint sauce
3 tbsp lemon juice
1½ tsp salt
1½ tsp paprika

Put all the ingredients in a food processor and mix to a smooth consistency. Best to do this in pulses until the mixture is to your liking.

PURIS

1kg atta (chapati flour)
vegetable oil, for frying

Place the flour in a large bowl and make a well in the centre. Slowly add cold water to make a fairly stiff dough and knead well. Leave the dough to rest for about 20 minutes. Make small balls the size of a plum and roll them out in rounds – or use a special puri press to save time. Heat the oil in a heavy pan or a karai. Drop in the puris a few at a time and fry until golden. Drain on kitchen paper and serve warm.

YOGHURT BOONDI

55g ready-made boondi
1 tsp salt and 1 tsp paprika
1 tsp lovage seeds and 1 tsp cumin seeds
handful of fresh coriander, chopped
500ml plain live yoghurt

Soak the boondi (fried droplets of besan batter) in warm water for about 10 minutes. When it is soft, drain, rinse in cold water and drain again. Stir the spices and coriander into the yoghurt, add the boondi and mix well. Chill before serving.

KEDGEREE

Great served with dishes like the curried salmon (see page 88) for special occasions. Mung beans can usually be used straight from the packet without being soaked.

SERVES 6–8

250g green mung beans
1 tsp salt
300g rice, washed well
1 tbsp clarified butter

Place the mung beans in a large saucepan and add enough boiling water to come to about 2.5cm above them. Add the salt, bring to the boil and simmer until the beans are half cooked. Add the rice and clarified butter and stir gently to mix. Top up with boiling water so that the level is again about 2.5cm above the contents. Bring to the boil and leave on a low heat until the rice is cooked and the liquid is absorbed.

Check on the rice by picking out a grain and gently squeezing it between your fingertips. If it still has a white centre, it is not quite cooked and needs a little longer. If all the liquid has already been absorbed, add a small amount to make a little steam to finish cooking the rice without burning. Once the rice is cooked, remove it from the heat. Use the handle of a ladle or palette knife to fluff up the rice – move it gently through the rice and around the sides of the pan. Do this only once.

To clarify butter, dice and slowly heat the butter in a small pan until it separates and the white solids sink to the bottom. Pour the clarified liquid into a dish, leaving the residue in the pan.

CHICKEN CURRY

A great chicken curry recipe from Harjinder. She says this tarka masala sauce is the base for many Punjabi dishes. Harjinder loves to cook dishes like this for her family and has even made videos of how to prepare her recipes for her children.

SERVES 6

1kg boneless chicken breasts, cut into big chunks

1½ tsp salt

1½ tsp ground black peppercorns and coriander seeds

¾ tsp garam masala (see page 90)

1 tsp paprika

1½ tsp turmeric

½ tsp red chilli flakes

2 fresh tomatoes, sliced

handful of fresh coriander, chopped

3 bay leaves

TARKA MASALA SAUCE

3 tbsp sunflower oil, ghee or olive oil

2 tsp cumin seeds

2 medium onions, peeled and chopped

1 head of garlic, cloves peeled and chopped

small tin of chopped tomatoes

5cm piece of root ginger, peeled and chopped

2 whole green chillies

Wash the chicken and drain it well. Start by making the tarka masala sauce. Heat the oil in a large pan until fairly hot, add the cumin seeds and fry for 10 seconds. Add the onions and fry until golden brown, then add the garlic and fry until slightly golden. Drain the tomatoes (keep the juice), and add them to the pan, then add the ginger and chillies and cook until the oil begins to separate.

Put the chicken, salt, spices and chilli flakes into the pan and cook over a fairly high heat. Keep turning the chicken and continue to cook until the meat is sealed and browned and the liquid has evaporated. Add the juice from the can of tomatoes and about 450ml of water, bring to the boil and simmer over a medium heat for about 15 minutes or until the chicken is tender. Add the fresh tomatoes about 3 minutes before the end of the cooking time.

Sprinkle in the fresh coriander and bay leaves and serve the curry with chapatis, boiled rice or puris.

RHODA'S CHICKEN CURRY

This recipe was given to us at one of the food fairs by a lady called Roz. It's a South African chicken curry that her mum Rhoda used to make and it's great. Give it a go.

SERVES 4–6

3 tbsp olive oil

1 large onion, peeled and sliced

6 green cardamom pods

4 cloves

2 large cinnamon sticks

1 tsp black mustard seeds (optional)

3 bay leaves

3 green chillies, seeded and chopped

1 tsp ground turmeric

2 tsp chilli powder

1 tsp ground cumin

1 tsp garam masala

1.5cm piece of root ginger, crushed

3 garlic cloves, crushed

a few curry leaves

750g–1kg chicken, skinned and cut into large chunks

1 level tsp salt

1 x 400g can of tomatoes

2 large potatoes, peeled and quartered

handful of fresh coriander, washed and chopped

Heat the oil in a large non-stick saucepan. Add the onion and fry gently until it is softened and browned. Add the cardamom, cloves, cinnamon, mustard seeds (if using), bay leaves and chillies and continue to fry gently. Take the pan off the heat and stir in the turmeric, chilli powder, cumin, garam masala, root ginger, garlic and curry leaves. Put the saucepan back on the heat, add the chicken and salt and mix together well.

Cover the pan and cook over a low heat to extract all the flavour from the spices. Add the tomatoes and continue to cook, stirring occasionally. Then add the potatoes and cook until the potatoes are done. Sprinkle in the chopped coriander and serve with basmati rice.

PAN HAGGERTY

Although traditionally a dish from the coalfields of northeast England,
this is not just for underground Geordies. It's a great one-pan supper and
just the job for eating in front of the telly when you want a bit of comfort.

SERVES 4–6

1 tbsp vegetable oil
250g streaky bacon rashers
6 medium potatoes, peeled and sliced
into thin rounds
2 onions, peeled and sliced
5 carrots, peeled and sliced
500ml chicken stock
150g Cheddar cheese, grated
salt and pepper to taste

A high-sided frying pan is best for making this. Heat the oil in the pan and fry the bacon until it starts to crisp and colour. Remove the rashers and set aside, leaving the fat and juices in the pan.

Place a layer of potatoes over the bottom of the pan. Add a layer of onion, then a layer of carrot, then a layer of bacon rashers. Season with freshly ground pepper. Repeat the layers, finishing with a layer of potatoes. Season with salt and pepper, but be careful not to add too much salt, as the bacon will be salty and the stock too.

Pour on the chicken stock and cover the pan with a lid if you have one or with foil. Leave it to simmer away for about 20 minutes or until the vegetables are tender.

When everything is cooked, preheat the grill. Uncover the pan, top with the grated cheese and grill until bubbling and golden. Serve straight from the pan into bowls, with some bread to mop up the yummy juices.

GREEN BEAN SOUP
(FEIJAO VERDE SOPA)

Jeni Candeias lives in Merseyside. She is British, but has a Portuguese husband, and she really loves to cook Portuguese dishes. Her family life centres around food and everyone sits down to eat an evening meal together. Jeni learned to cook traditional dishes from her mother-in-law, Maria, and has added her own twist to some. She's also introduced her Portuguese relatives to British favourites, like the Sunday roast. The Portuguese are great soup eaters and this is one of the most popular.

SERVES 8

½ medium onion, peeled and chopped
2–3 garlic cloves, peeled and chopped
400g potatoes, peeled and chopped
4 carrots, 2 roughly chopped, 2 sliced
1.2 litres chicken stock
2 tbsp olive oil
200g green beans, sliced diagonally
100g chorizo, cut into slices 1cm thick
salt and pepper

Put the onion, garlic, potatoes and the roughly chopped carrots in a large pan and add the chicken stock and olive oil.

Bring everything to the boil and cook until the vegetables are tender. Pour into a blender and blitz until smooth. Pour the mixture back into the pan and add the green beans, sliced carrots and chorizo. Season to taste and cook until the beans are tender. Stir regularly as the chorizo may stick to the bottom of the pan.

Serve with crusty bread and freshly ground black pepper.

PORTUGUESE FISH & CHIPS
(BACALHAU A BRAS)

Another recipe from Jeni and this one really convinced us about salt cod, a Portuguese staple. This is a great supper dish and her kids love it – they've grown up with her version of fish and chips. You need to start the day before by soaking the salt cod.

SERVES 5

1.3kg salt cod
1 tbsp olive oil
½ onion, peeled and diced
1–2 garlic cloves, peeled and chopped
3 eggs, beaten
vegetable oil, for deep frying
1.2kg potatoes, cut into matchstick chips
good handful of chopped parsley
black pepper

Rinse the salt cod, place it in a bowl and cover with cold water. Leave it to soak for 24 hours, changing the water at least twice.

The next day, drain the cod well and put it in a large pan. Pour in enough cold water to cover, bring it to the boil and cook for 20 minutes or so or until the fish is tender and flaky. Leave to cool, then separate into flakes and remove any skin and bones.

Heat the olive oil in a large pan and cook the onion and garlic until softened. Add the salt cod and the beaten eggs and stir over a gentle heat until the eggs are cooked. Meanwhile, heat the vegetable oil in a deep-fat fryer or large pan and cook the chips until golden. Add them to the pan with the fish and sprinkle with the chopped parsley. Season with black pepper and serve with a tomato and onion salad.

This can also be eaten cold.

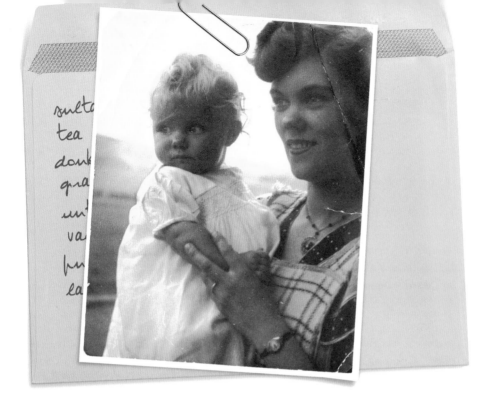

TRADITIONAL RICE PUDDING

We love this – a real comforting taste of childhood. A top tip from Si's mam: soak some sultanas in builders' tea for 10 minutes and add them to the rice pudding for some special little explosions of flavour. On high days and holidays, serve this with a dollop of clotted cream and your favourite jam.

SERVES 6

100g sultanas
hot tea
1.3 litres full-fat milk
300ml double cream
200g pudding rice
100g golden granulated sugar
good sprinkling of freshly ground nutmeg
1 vanilla pod

First, put the sultanas in a bowl and cover them with hot tea. Leave for 10 minutes and then drain the sultanas and discard the tea.

Preheat the oven to 160°C/Gas 2–3. Pour the milk and cream into a big casserole dish or a rice pudding dish. Add the rice, sugar and nutmeg and stir well. Split the vanilla pod and scrape out the seeds, then add the seeds and pod to the dish. Stir in the soaked sultanas.

Cover the dish with a lid or some foil, place in the oven and bake for about an hour and a half. Uncover and bake for another 20 minutes so a golden skin forms… some say that's the best bit.

PORTUGUESE RICE PUDDING

This is a recipe from the Alentejo area, where Jeni's mother-in-law lives.

SERVES 6

250g long-grain rice
25g lard
300ml milk
250g caster sugar
1 cinnamon stick
zest of 1 lemon
3 egg yolks
ground cinnamon

Wash and drain the rice and put it in a pan with about 450ml of salted water and the lard. When the rice has just started to cook, gradually add the milk and the sugar with the stick of cinnamon and lemon zest. Stir continuously.

Once the rice is not crunchy or too mushy, remove the cinnamon stick. Take the pan off the heat and add the egg yolks. Stir them in thoroughly before putting the pan on a low heat so the eggs can cook through. Serve hot or cold with a sprinkling of powdered cinnamon.

BALINESE RICE PUDDING

There are so many kinds of rice pudding – it's something that crops up all over the world. Here is an amazing Balinese recipe with black rice. The ingredients sound exotic but they are available in most Thai shops. Screwpine or pandanus leaves have a sweet flavour and scent and are used in many Southeast Asian rice dishes and desserts. If you can't get the leaves, you can use pandan essence or even vanilla essence.

SERVES 6

300g black glutinous rice
170g palm sugar, grated
2 screwpine leaves or
2 drops of pandan or vanilla essence
450ml coconut milk
pinch of salt
fresh coconut to garnish

Wash the rice and leave it to soak in cold water overnight. Next day, drain the rice and put it in a saucepan with about 1.5 litres of water. Bring it to the boil and cook until the rice is soft. Add the sugar (more or less, according to taste) and a screwpine leaf or drop of essence. Continue to boil until the rice is cooked through, then leave to cool for a while, then garnish with fresh coconut.

Pour the coconut milk into another pan, add the remaining leaf or essence and the salt and cook until thickened. Serve with the rice. This pudding looks spectacular when the white milk is poured over the dark rice.

POTTED SHRIMPS

These make Sunday teatime special. You'll need four ramekin dishes.

SERVES 4

200g unsalted butter
splash of lemon juice
zest of ½ lemon
½ tsp mace
pinch of cayenne pepper
200g brown shrimps, peeled
curly parsley, chopped
salt and black pepper

First you need to clarify the butter. Just bring it to the boil in a small pan, then remove it from the heat and skim off the foam. Pour out the clarified butter, leaving the milky residue behind, and mix it with the lemon juice and zest, mace, cayenne and seasoning.

Divide the shrimps between the ramekins and pour a quarter of the spiced butter mixture into each. Add some chopped parsley if you like.

Place the ramekins in the fridge until set solid. Serve with a side salad, lemon wedges and melba toast.

MELBA TOAST

Serve this with potted shrimps or prawn cocktail.

SERVES 4

1 white loaf or
8 slices of white sliced bread

THE PROPER WAY
Preheat the oven to 180°C/Gas 4. Trim the crusts off a good white loaf and cut into wafer-thin slices. Place on a baking tray and bake for about 10 minutes until crispy.

THE QUICK WAY
Take some white sliced bread and pop it into the toaster. Split the slices of toast in two before serving.

SPAGHETTI ALLA CARBONARA

A classic quick supper dish that you will want to make again and again. This is our version and it's a proper carbonara – not the creamy custard effort with bits of tired boiled ham you get in many establishments. You can use Pecorino cheese if you want a slightly more mellow flavour.

SERVES 4

1 tbsp extra virgin olive oil
250g pancetta or very smoky bacon,
cut into tiny cubes
100g unsalted butter
150ml dry white wine
4 whole eggs
2 egg yolks
100g Parmesan cheese, grated,
plus extra for serving
400g spaghetti
salt and freshly ground black pepper

First, warm the oil in a frying pan and fry the pancetta or bacon slowly until golden. All the lovely smoky flavours will leech into the oil. Add half the butter, then the wine and simmer for a couple of minutes.

In a bowl, beat the whole eggs with the egg yolks and add the cheese. Season, but go easy on the salt because the bacon or pancetta will be salty.

Cook the spaghetti according to the instructions on the packet. Drain the pasta, add to the warm pancetta or bacon mixture and mix until the pasta is nicely coated. Stir in the eggs and cheese – the heat from the pasta will cook the egg.

Stir in the remaining butter, check the seasoning and serve right away with some extra grated cheese and a crunchy salad.

For an even quicker supper dish with a different taste, use cured ham, such as Parma or Serrano, instead of bacon or pancetta. Just cut the ham into small pieces, add it to the pasta with the eggs and warm it through. Serve at once.

THE GURKHAS

The Gurkhas have been part of the British Army for 200 years and are renowned for their bravery in battle. 'Better to die than be a coward', is their motto. The soldiers come from Nepal and northern India and take their name from an eighth-century warrior saint named Guru Gorakhnath. A group from the 2nd Signal Regiment, Imphal Barracks, came to one of our recipe fairs and cooked us some amazing food.

MUTTON CURRY WITH SAUCE
(BHUTEK O DUMBA KO MASU)

This is a great dish that the Gurkhas cooked up for us at the recipe fair.

SERVES 10

1.2kg boneless leg of mutton
250g fresh tomatoes
50g fresh coriander
4 garlic cloves
50g fresh root ginger
250g white onions
75–100ml olive oil
50g garam masala
200g tomato passata
salt to taste

For an extra spicy flavour, add fresh chillies to the mutton.

Cut the mutton into 1.5cm cubes. Blanch the tomatoes, then peel, de-seed and cut them into small dice. Wash the fresh coriander and chop it finely.

Peel the garlic, ginger and onions and chop them very finely until you have a paste – or blitz in a food processor. Heat the oil in a large heavy-based pan until a blue haze appears, then add the ginger, onion and garlic paste and fry for 5 minutes. Add the mutton and fry for a further 5 minutes, then stir in the garam masala, tomato passata, fresh tomatoes and a pinch of salt. Reduce the heat, cover the saucepan and cook for 30–40 minutes.

At the end of this time, check that the mutton is fully cooked and tender and adjust the seasoning. Serve in a heated dish and garnish with the fresh coriander. For a proper feast, serve with basmati rice, dhal (lentils), aludam potatoes, naan bread and Gurkha sesame chutney.

CURRIED POTATOES (ALUDAM)

Serve this with the mutton curry opposite for a Gurkha-style feast.

SERVES 10

2kg white potatoes, peeled
200g white onions, peeled and sliced
50g fresh green chillies, sliced
4 garlic cloves
50g fresh root ginger
50g fresh coriander
150ml rapeseed oil, for frying
1 tsp ground cumin
1 tsp ground turmeric
1 tsp garam masala
100g tomato passata
salt and pepper

Cut the potatoes into small dice (about 1cm) and blanch them in salted water until partly cooked. Mix the sliced onions with the green chillies. Peel and finely dice the garlic and ginger, then add them to the onion and chilli mix. Wash and finely chop the fresh coriander.

Heat the oil in a large pan until a blue haze appears. Add the onion, garlic and ginger mixture, fry for a few minutes, then add all the remaining spices, tomato passata and a pinch of salt. Fry for a further 5 minutes. Add the potatoes and sauté until all the ingredients have combined and the potato is cooked. Adjust the seasoning to taste and garnish with some fresh coriander.

SESAME CHUTNEY

This is a perfect accompaniment to any lamb or mutton curry.

170g fresh tomatoes
30g sesame seeds
110g cucumber, peeled and diced
170g white onions, peeled and diced
60g green chillies, seeded and diced
juice and zest of 1 medium lemon
55g fresh coriander, washed and finely chopped
½ tsp salt

Blanch the tomatoes, then peel, de-seed and cut them into small dice. Grind the sesame seeds. Mix all the ingredients together, reserving a spoonful of chopped coriander. Add salt to taste, transfer to a chilled bowl to serve and garnish with the rest of the fresh coriander.

Birthday treats

SUMMER BERRY TRIFLE

This fresh fruit trifle may take a little time to make, but it's worth the effort. We like to include the jelly, but if you're short of time, leave it out and the trifle will still be delicious. You can vary the booze to suit the jelly flavour – for example, limoncello with lemon jelly or cassis with blackcurrant.

SERVES 8

1 x 170g jam Swiss roll
5 tbsp cream sherry
75g blueberries
100g raspberries
150g strawberries, hulled and halved
135g packet raspberry or strawberry jelly

CUSTARD

300ml whole milk
300ml double cream
1 vanilla pod, slit lengthways
and seeds removed
2 tbsp cornflour
4 large free-range egg yolks
75g caster sugar

TOPPING

flaked almonds
300ml double cream

Cut the Swiss roll into 12 slices and arrange over the base and a short way up the sides of a glass trifle bowl. Put the remaining slices in the middle. Spoon the sherry over the sponge slices and let it soak in. Scatter the fresh fruit on top of the soaked sponge. Make the jelly according to the instructions on the packet and pour it over the fruit. Cover the dish with clingfilm and leave in the fridge for about 2 hours for the jelly to set.

Meanwhile, make the custard. Pour the milk and cream into a medium saucepan and add the vanilla pod and seeds. Bring to the boil, taking care that it doesn't boil over. Remove from the heat and leave to infuse for 15 minutes. Remove the vanilla pod.

Blend the cornflour with 2 tablespoons of cold water and set aside. Whisk the egg yolks and sugar in a large bowl until pale and thick. Gradually stir in the milk and cream mixture until smooth. Pour the mixture back into the saucepan and return to the heat. Cook over a low heat for 8–10 minutes, stirring constantly, until the custard is thick enough to coat the back of a spoon – it should have the consistency of single cream. Do not overheat or the eggs may scramble!

Give the cornflour mixture a stir, then mix quickly into the custard. Cook for 1–2 minutes longer, until the custard is well thickened and smooth, stirring constantly. Remove from the heat and pour into a bowl placed over another bowl filled with iced water. Cover the surface of the custard with clingfilm to prevent a skin forming and leave until it is cold.

Remove the clingfilm, stir the custard and gently pour it onto the set jelly. Return the trifle dish to the fridge for another 30 minutes or until the custard is lightly set. To prepare the topping, lightly toast the almonds in a dry frying pan over a low heat until golden, turning regularly. Set aside to cool.

Whip the cream until it forms soft peaks. Spoon the whipped cream over the custard, starting at the sides of the bowl before working your way into the middle. Scatter over the almonds, cover and return to the fridge until ready to serve.

Thickening the custard with a little cornflour stops the cream topping from sinking into the custard.

CURRIED MUTTON
WITH RICE & PEAS & FRIED DUMPLINGS

Connie Smith runs an amazing Caribbean takeaway called Connie's Nine Mile in Leicester and she serves up the tastiest food. She learned to cook from her granny and great-granny back in Jamaica and came to Britain in the 1960s. She cooked a dish for us that features at every Caribbean social event, from birthdays and weddings to christenings. It's often referred to as 'big peoples food' but is enjoyed by young and old alike. Rice and peas is a great accompaniment – Connie explained to us that it's always called rice and peas, whatever kind of dried pea or bean you use.

SERVES 6

CURRIED MUTTON

900g mutton

1 medium onion, finely chopped

2 garlic cloves, finely chopped

2 spring onions (scallions), roughly chopped

1 Scotch bonnet pepper, finely chopped

2½ tbsp curry powder

1 sprig of fresh thyme

1½ tsp of salt

½ tsp ground black pepper

2 carrots, peeled and roughly chopped

2 celery sticks, roughly chopped

1 tbsp vegetable oil

RICE AND PEAS

225g kidney beans, soaked overnight, or a can of beans

1 fresh coconut or a can of coconut milk

2 whole spring onions (scallions)

1 sprig of fresh thyme

2 tsp salt

900g easy-cook long grain rice

1 Scotch bonnet pepper

1 knob of butter or margarine

Wash the meat and cut it into cubes. Place it in a large dish and season with the onion, garlic, spring onions, Scotch bonnet, curry powder, thyme, salt and pepper, then add the chopped carrots and celery. Leave to marinate for at least 2 hours but ideally overnight.

When the meat has marinated, heat a heavy-based pan with the oil. Remove the meat from the seasoning and brown it in the pan in batches. Set the seasoning aside for later. Then put all the meat in the pan, cover it with boiling water and simmer for 2 hours or until tender.

Add the seasoning and simmer for another 30 minutes, adding more water if necessary. At the end of the cooking time, the mutton mixture should be reduced to a tender stew.

RICE AND PEAS

If using dried beans, soak them overnight in cold water. The next day, drain them, place in a large saucepan and cover with fresh water. Bring to the boil and boil for 10 minutes, then simmer until the beans are tender.

If you want to use fresh coconut instead of canned coconut milk, grate the flesh of the coconut into a bowl. Pour 150ml of boiling water over it, leave to stand for 1 hour, then squeeze through a damp cloth.

Add the coconut milk to the beans, with the spring onions, thyme and salt. Bring to the boil and add the rice and Scotch bonnet (whole, not chopped) and stir. The water should be just covering the rice.

FRIED DUMPLINGS

700g se lf-raising flour
½ tsp salt
30g butter or margarine
300ml oil, for frying

Reduce to a very low heat and simmer for 30 minutes by which time the rice should be tender and the water absorbed. If the rice is still hard, add a little more water and continue to simmer until cooked.

Remove the whole Scotch bonnet and spring onion. Add a knob of butter, then simmer for a further 5 minutes. Serve hot with curried mutton and dumplings.

FRIED DUMPLINGS

Sieve the flour into a bowl and stir in the salt. Cut the butter into small cubes and add to the flour.

Add water a little at a time and work it into the mixture to make a dough – if the water is added too quickly the mixture may not bind properly. Knead the dough until it is smooth. Divide into small balls about 5cm in diameter, then flatten the balls so that they are about 2cm thick.

Heat the oil over a low heat and fry the dumplings until they are golden brown all over – about 5 minutes. Place them on some kitchen towel to absorb the excess oil and serve hot.

SKY (SEXY) JUICE

Connie says you can make this drink into a light meal by adding some vanilla nourishment powder. Or you can make it with Guinness instead of pineapple juice!

1 x 1 litre carton of pineapple juice
½ can of condensed milk (or to taste)
grated nutmeg
vanilla essence

Whizz up the pineapple juice and the condensed milk – add more or less according to how sweet you like your treats. Add a grating of nutmeg and a few drops of vanilla essence.

SATURDAY SOUP

Another recipe from Connie. This is what she told us about this one: 'When I was growing up in Jamaica, it was a tradition that every Saturday we'd all eat soup made from various meats, an assortment of Caribbean vegetables and soft spinner dumplings. It was the only thing cooked on a Saturday and was made in a huge pot to serve all the members of the family and any friends visiting. This tradition still goes on today, not only in Jamaica but also throughout the Caribbean islands and with many families living in the UK. This is my version of Saturday soup, just like mama used to make.'

SERVES 10–12

1 chicken carcass for stock
750g boned chicken thigh meat
450g pumpkin
1 cho-cho (or squash)
450g soft yam
450g potatoes
225g sweet potatoes
2 sweetcorn (on the cob)
2 spring onions (scallions)
1 Scotch bonnet pepper, finely chopped
2 sprigs of fresh thyme
1 packet of chicken noodle soup
salt and black pepper to taste
cornflour (optional)

SPINNER DUMPLINGS

450g plain flour
½ tsp salt

Half fill a large saucepan with water and bring it to the boil. Add the chicken carcass and cook it for 1 hour. Discard the bones, add the chicken meat, cut into pieces, and cook for another 30 minutes until the chicken is cooked. Skim any froth from the top of the stock.

Wash and peel the vegetables, except the Scotch bonnet, and cut them into bite-size pieces – not too small. Add them to the stock, bring it back to the boil and simmer for another 30 minutes, stirring occasionally.

Meanwhile, sift the flour and salt into a bowl. Add enough cold water to make a soft dough and knead for 5 minutes. Roll the dough in the palm of your hand to make sausage-shaped dumplings about 6cm long and 1.5cm thick.

Add the dumplings, Scotch bonnet, thyme and chicken noodle soup mix to the saucepan and season to taste. Stir and simmer for 15–20 minutes, then serve hot. The soup should be of a medium consistency so add some boiling water if it's too thick. If it's too watery, add some cornflour, stir well and simmer for another 5 minutes.

COTTAGE PIE
WITH CHEESY MASH

We both think that cottage or shepherd's pie is the perfect birthday tea – these were a real treat for us when we were lads. Our special version of shepherd's pie is made just the same way as below, but with two parts minced lamb to one part haggis for a good gamey flavour.

SERVES 4–5

1 tbsp sunflower oil
1 large onion, chopped
2 celery sticks, stringed and diced
2 medium-large carrots, peeled and diced
2 garlic cloves, finely chopped
500g lean minced beef
150ml red wine
2 tbsp plain flour
250ml beef stock (fresh or from a cube)
2 tbsp tomato purée
½ tsp mixed dried herbs
1 bay leaf
splash of Worcestershire sauce
salt and freshly ground black pepper

TOPPING

800g medium potatoes, peeled and cut
into even-sized pieces
40g butter, cubed
3 tbsp milk
100g good mature Cheddar cheese, grated
salt and freshly ground black pepper

Heat the sunflower oil in a large deep sauté pan or saucepan and gently fry the onion, celery and carrots for 8 minutes or until the onions are softened and lightly coloured. Add the garlic and cook for 2 minutes more. Stir all the vegetables occasionally to prevent them from becoming too brown.

Tip the mince into the pan and cook with the vegetables for 5 minutes or until no pinkness remains, stirring regularly to break up the meat. Pour the wine into the pan and cook until all the liquid evaporates, then sprinkle over the flour and stir well for a minute or two.

Gradually stir the beef stock into the pan. Add 250ml of cold water, the tomato purée and herbs. Bring to a gentle simmer, cover and cook over a low heat for 25–30 minutes, stirring occasionally, until the mince is tender and the sauce has thickened. If it starts to look too dry, add some more stock or water. Season with Worcestershire sauce and salt and pepper to taste. Remove from the heat and spoon the mince mixture into a 1.5 litre ovenproof dish. Leave to stand while you get the mash ready.

Boil the potatoes until they are very soft. Drain well, then return them to the saucepan and add the butter, milk and cheese. Mash until smooth and creamy and season to taste. Preheat the oven to 200°C/Gas 6.

Spoon the potato over the mince mixture, working around the edge before heading towards the middle. When all the mince is covered, rough up the surface with a fork and place the dish on a baking tray. Bake in the centre of the oven for about 25 minutes or until the potatoes are golden brown and the filling is bubbling. Serve with freshly cooked green beans or shredded Savoy cabbage. And don't forget the ketchup!

STUFFED VINE LEAVES (DOLMADES/KOUBEBIA)

In Birmingham, we met Ira Phedon, whose family is from Cyprus. Ira loves to cook for her large family and admits she spends much of her time cooking for the masses. This is what she says about her version of stuffed vine leaves: 'These are a bit fiddly to make but well worth it, I promise you! It goes without saying that tender, fresh vine leaves are better in flavour and texture than the preserved ones, but I realise that the fresh variety can be difficult to come by. So if you know anyone who has a vine growing in their garden, get friendly! You can wrap the leaves in clingfilm in batches of about 35 and freeze them so that you have fresh leaves all year round. But don't worry if you can only get the preserved leaves. You'll still end up making the tastiest "koubebia" you've ever tasted. If you do use leaves preserved in brine, though, do make sure you wash them really well. These stuffed vine leaves are wonderful eaten with a nice Greek salad (don't forget the dips) and some warm pitta bread. Or serve with roast chicken as an alternative to your usual veg and gravy.'

MAKES ABOUT 30

30–35 vine leaves (about 200g)
500g pork mince
1 large onion, peeled and finely chopped
about 60g fresh flat-leaf parsley, finely chopped
100g long-grain white rice, rinsed and left to drain
1 chicken stock cube
½ x 400g can of good-quality chopped tomatoes
1 very generous tbsp tomato purée
juice of 1 large lemon
120ml extra virgin olive oil
1 tbsp dried mint
½ tsp ground cinnamon
salt and freshly ground black pepper
1 heaped tsp butter

Whether your vine leaves are fresh, frozen or preserved, place them in a wide shallow bowl and pour over enough boiling water to cover them. Leave them to soften and/or thaw for 3–4 minutes. Drain the water and gently squeeze the leaves between your hands to remove as much liquid as possible. Remember that the leaves are quite delicate, so don't squeeze too hard. Wrap them in some kitchen towel to absorb any excess moisture.

The next part is nice and easy. Place all the ingredients, except the butter, vine leaves and 2 tablespoons of the olive oil, into a large mixing bowl. Make sure you crumble the stock cube well between your fingers so that it gets distributed, then start to knead the mixture with your hands until everything is thoroughly combined.

Drizzle the remaining olive oil into the base of a medium-sized saucepan. Gently unravel the vine leaves and use 3 or 4 to line the base of the saucepan so that the stuffed leaves don't stick.

It's best to prepare the vine leaves on a plate rather than a completely flat surface, so that the plate can catch the juices.

Later, when you've finished preparing the dolmades, you can pour any leftover juice from the plate or the mixing bowl over the stuffed vine leaves in the saucepan.

Place a vine leaf (top side down) on the plate. Carefully spoon about a tablespoon of the meat mixture onto the bottom end of the leaf, close to the stem. Now fold the left and right sides of the leaf over the filling and roll it up quite tightly (but not too much so) from the base, into a neat cylinder.

As you stuff the vine leaves, place them into the saucepan, one at a time, working round from the sides of the saucepan to the centre and packing them in quite tightly. Depending on the diameter of the saucepan, you will probably have two layers. Pour over about 75ml of cold water and any juice remaining on your plate or mixing bowl and dot with the butter.

If you are left with any spare leaves, layer them over the top of the dolmades.

Finally, find a plate that fits snugly into the saucepan and place it over the vine leaves to keep them in place. Put the saucepan over a medium heat and when the liquid starts to boil, turn the heat right down, cover the saucepan with a lid and leave to simmer gently for about 45 minutes.

About halfway through the cooking time, remove the lid and partially cover for the rest of the time. When the dolmades are ready, remove the saucepan from the heat and clamp the lid back on.

Always allow at least 45 minutes resting time so the juices are fully absorbed. Then the dolmades are ready to serve.

Obviously, vine leaves can vary quite a lot in size, so reduce or increase the quantity of stuffing to suit your leaves.

BASTICHIO

Another one from Ira and one of her favourite Greek dishes. This is what she says about it:
'Bastichio is the name that I grew up with, but some villages in Cyprus call this dish "macaronia tou fournou", which loosely translated means "baked pasta". There is a lot more to it than that, however! I like to describe it as the Greek version of lasagne and I think it's even nicer if that's possible, but obviously I'm biased. It's also one of those ever-popular dishes that is great for any buffet or celebratory meal. It can be prepared the day before up to the point of baking and refrigerating, so that all of the hard work is out of the way and you can bake it fresh on the day you're going to eat it – great for when you've got friends and family coming round! It goes without saying that a big juicy Greek salad goes really well with this one.' This is how Ira makes bastichio.

SERVES 8 (or 6 Greeks!)

MIDDLE LAYER: MEAT SAUCE

2 tbsp vegetable oil
500g pork mince
5 tbsp olive oil
2 medium onions, peeled and finely chopped
2 fat garlic cloves, peeled and finely chopped
1 heaped tsp ground cinnamon
2 heaped tbsp dried mint
1 chicken stock cube
big handful of fresh flat-leaf parsley, finely chopped
about 500g tomato passata
good sprinkling of paprika
½ tsp sugar
salt and freshly ground black pepper

BOTTOM LAYER: PASTA

1 chicken or vegetable stock cube
350g penne rigate
pinch of grated or ground nutmeg
1 heaped tbsp butter
about 200g Greek halloumi cheese, grated
2 egg whites from large eggs, lightly beaten
8 tbsp béchamel sauce

You will need a rectangular oven dish measuring about 33 x 29cm and 7cm deep.

Even though the meat sauce forms the middle layer of the bastichio, I always prepare it first and leave it to simmer gently while I get on with the rest of it. The way I like to fry mince may be different to what you're used to: basically I like to drain away the fat before adding any of the other ingredients, so that I don't lose any of those gorgeous flavours.

Begin by heating the oil in a large saucepan and then add the mince. Fry the mince over a medium heat for about 5 minutes until it browns, stirring most of the time to break up any lumps and stop it from sticking to the bottom of the saucepan. Now, drain away most of the fat. There's no need to sieve it, just gingerly tilt the pan over the sink and use the lid or a slotted spoon as a barrier to stop the mince from falling out.

Return the pan to the heat, add the olive oil, onions and garlic and fry for a couple of minutes. Add the cinnamon, mint, crumbled stock cube, parsley, passata, paprika, sugar and a seasoning of salt and freshly ground black pepper and give it all a really good stir.

Partly cover with a lid and leave the meat to simmer on a low heat, stirring every now and then, until about 10 minutes before it's time to assemble the bastichio.

Bring a large pan of lightly salted water to the boil and add the stock cube. Add the penne and cook according to the instructions on the packet.

TOP LAYER: BÉCHAMEL

200g butter, melted and cooled
½ tsp grated or ground nutmeg
pinch of ground cinnamon
pinch of salt
2 egg yolks from large eggs
1.2 litres milk
200ml crème fraîche
150g cornflour
about 100g Greek halloumi cheese,
grated

While the meat and the pasta are simmering, start on the béchamel sauce. In another saucepan, place the cooled, melted butter, nutmeg, cinnamon, salt and egg yolks and gently whisk until well combined – a balloon whisk is best for this. Add the milk and crème fraîche and whisk again to incorporate. Set aside for a few moments while you attend to the pasta.

When the pasta is ready, drain most of the liquid away reserving about 2 or 3 tablespoons. Pour the pasta with the reserved liquid into the base of your oven dish and while it's hot and steaming, add the nutmeg, butter and the halloumi cheese and mix really well. Set aside for a couple of minutes to cool down slightly and then stir in the egg whites.

Preheat the oven to 180°C/Gas 4. To finish the béchamel, add the cornflour, a tablespoon at a time, whisking as each spoonful goes in. Place the saucepan over a medium heat and start to whisk for England – don't stop until the sauce is completely ready. It will look slightly unattractive and lumpy at the start, but don't panic as it will turn into a beautiful, glossy sauce when it's finished. As the sauce starts to thicken, turn the heat down slightly and stir a bit harder, so that it doesn't catch the bottom of the pan. When the béchamel starts to bubble gently, remove from the heat and stir 8 tablespoons into the pasta.

Take the slightly cooled meat sauce and spread it all over the pasta to cover the meat completely. Finally, spread the lovely béchamel over the meat sauce and sprinkle generously with the grated halloumi cheese.

Place the bastichio in the top third of the oven for about 40 minutes until it's nicely browned. Leave to stand for about an hour before dishing up (or preferably a bit longer if you can resist) as it allows the juices to settle and absorb, and makes it easier to cut into pieces. It's definitely worth the wait.

If you have prepared the bastichio for cooking the next day, pop it in fridge once it is cool. Just remember to take it out a couple of hours before you want to cook it. It will need a longer cooking time – about 1 hour – to make sure it is brown and bubbling and the meat is thoroughly reheated.

Like a lot of Greek food, bastichio tastes best served lukewarm, rather than piping hot.

VERY SPECIAL CHOCOLATE MOUSSE TRIO

Chocolate mousse must be one of the most popular of all desserts. We love it – but we are talking mousse with good chocolate, really decadent and luxurious. This recipe is from Si's Auntie Hilda who made it for his mam and dad's silver wedding anniversary and we have tinkered a little to make it super special. Using three different chocolates – dark, milk and white – takes this dish to another dimension, and there's an optional hit of Drambuie in the white chocolate part. Auntie Hilda would be proud. You'll need some nice glasses for serving the mousse.

SERVES 6–8

750ml whipping cream
200g dark chocolate, broken into pieces
200g milk chocolate, broken into pieces
200g white chocolate, broken into pieces
150g unsalted butter, divided into
3 x 50g pieces
3 egg yolks
1 big splash of Drambuie
extra dark chocolate for grating on top
(optional)

First whip the cream until it is firm and put it in the fridge to chill while you deal with the chocolate.

Set up 3 bain maries – that's 3 pudding basins over 3 pans of gently boiling water. The mission is to melt the 3 types of chocolate slowly. Place one kind of chocolate in each bowl. Add 50g of butter, cut into cubes, to each bowl. Let the chocolate and butter melt gently on their own – do not stir. Once melted, take the pans off the heat, stir with a fork to mix the butter and chocolate together, then leave to cool.

Once the chocolate and butter mixtures are cool enough, about blood temperature, stir an egg yolk into each bowl. Be patient here. If the chocolate is still too hot the eggs will scramble and we don't want that.

Bring out the whipped cream and divide into three. Into one portion, mix a good splash of Drambuie and fold that into the white chocolate with a spatula. Fold the other portions of cream into the dark chocolate and the milk chocolate.

Now you have 3 different kinds of chocolate mousse. Take the glasses that you are going to use for serving and spoon in some of the milk chocolate mousse. Layer on a spoonful of the Drambuie and white chocolate mousse, then finish with the dark chocolate mixture. Top with some grated dark chocolate if you like.

Refrigerate for at least 2 hours before serving. Pudding doesn't get much more special than this.

SAUSAGE PLAIT

Yvonne Langford from Digby, Lincolnshire, showed us some great recipes. Yvonne's grandma was a cook in a big country house and her grandad cooked for the Australian army so she has a real background in food. She herself trained as a chef and spent 30 years in catering. We are of the firm opinion that no birthday party is complete without a sausage roll, but they are the most abused item in British cooking. Yvonne's version – a sausage plait – is a winner so give it a try.

SERVES 6–8

PASTRY
450g plain flour
2 pinches of salt
140g lard, diced
140g margarine, diced
1 egg, beaten, and a little milk

FILLING
500g good quality sausage meat
2 medium onions, peeled and finely chopped
2 tsp mixed herbs
salt and black pepper

Start by making the pastry. Mix the flour and salt, then add the diced lard and margarine. Stir the fat in with a knife – do not rub in – and add a little cold water to make a stiff dough.

Roll the dough out to a narrow strip on a floured surface. Then fold it into 3 and turn it 90 degrees clockwise so that one of the open ends is towards you. Roll out and turn again. Repeat this 3 times, then cover the pastry and leave it to rest for about 15 minutes. Roll out into a rectangle ready for filling. (In hot weather, chill the pastry in the fridge or a cool place for 20–30 minutes before using.) You can, of course, use a packet of puff pastry if you prefer.

Preheat the oven to 230°C/Gas 8. Mix the sausage meat with the onions and add the mixed herbs and seasoning. Place the rectangle of pastry on a greased non-stick baking tray. Place the sausage mixture down the centre of the pastry, leaving a 5cm border down each side.

Working down each side, cut strips from the mixture to the edge of the pastry at a 45° angle at 2.5cm intervals. Carefully plait these strips across the sausage filling, working alternately left to right, then right to left. When the plaiting is complete, brush the pastry with a mixture of beaten egg and milk. Place in the oven and bake for about 30 minutes or until golden brown. Great hot or cold – just slice as required.

MANCHESTER TART

This used to be a school dinner favourite. We love it and Yvonne's version with banana is especially good. Yvonne told us that she used to keep her recipes secret, but is now happy to share them so that they don't disappear.

SERVES 6

PASTRY
450g self-raising flour
pinch of salt
110g lard
110g margarine
55g sugar

FILLING
3 tbsp custard powder
3 tbsp sugar
850ml milk
200g strawberry jam
3 large bananas, sliced
3 tbsp desiccated coconut

To make the pastry, mix the flour and salt in bowl, then rub in the lard and margarine until the mixture has a crumbly texture. Mix in the sugar. Using a knife, mix in a little cold water until a stiff dough is formed. Turn the dough out onto a floured worktop and roll it out to fit your flan tin. Lay the pastry over the tin, taking care to push it well into the sides. Trim off any excess.

Preheat the oven to 190°C/Gas 5. Put a circle of greaseproof paper over the pastry and pour in some baking beans or rice to keep it from rising. Bake for 15–20 minutes, then take the pastry out of the oven and leave it to cool. Remove the greaseproof paper and baking beans.

Put the custard powder and sugar in a bowl, add 2 tablespoons of the milk and mix to a smooth paste. Pour the rest of the milk into a saucepan and heat until nearly boiling, then pour this onto the custard mix, stirring well. Return the custard to the saucepan and bring to the boil over a gentle heat. Cook, stirring continuously, until the mixture thickens. Take off the heat and leave to cool.

Spread the jam on the base of the baked pastry case and add the sliced bananas. Pour the custard on top of the bananas and chill in the fridge overnight. Before serving, top with toasted coconut. To prepare this, put the desiccated coconut on a baking tray. Heat up the grill and place the coconut under the grill to toast. Watch the coconut carefully as it burns easily. Sprinkle the coconut on top of the custard and serve the tart with a jug of cream.

SNOW QUEEN

This recipe comes from Si's mother-in-law, Margaret. It's simple to prepare but really wows the taste buds. You'll need one of those jars of stem ginger in sugar syrup, which you can find in the supermarket or a good deli. It's worth hunting one out because it makes all the difference. Enjoy! We have on numerous occasions.

SERVES 4 GENEROUSLY

500ml double cream
2 tbsp brandy
1 tbsp caster sugar
1 tbsp chopped stem ginger, plus extra for garnish
1 tbsp stem ginger syrup (from the jar)
150g meringues
½ tsp groundnut oil
chocolate sauce or grated dark chocolate to serve

Pour the cream into a bowl and whisk until stiff – be careful not to overwhip it though, or it will split. Gently fold in the brandy, sugar, chopped ginger and ginger syrup until evenly distributed through the cream. Check for sweetness and add a touch more sugar or syrup if you want it sweeter. Roughly break up the meringues by hand – you need nice chunks, not dust – and fold them into the cream. This is your snow queen!

Lightly grease a 600ml pudding basin or an ice cream bomb mould with the groundnut oil. Spoon the mixture into the basin or mould and cover with foil, then clingfilm. Place in the freezer for 8 hours.

When you are nearly ready to serve, turn the snow queen out onto a serving plate and place it in the fridge for 15 minutes to soften a little. Sprinkle with extra stem ginger and top with some chocolate sauce or grated dark chocolate.

CHOCOLATE SAUCE

200g dark chocolate, broken into squares
2 tbsp golden syrup
55g butter, diced
small carton of single cream

Place a bowl over a pan of simmering water and add all the ingredients. Keep over a gentle heat until everything has melted, then stir and pour over your queen!

WELSH GRIDDLE CAKES

A friend of ours, whose family has made these griddle cakes for years, gave us this recipe.
In Argentina, we have eaten these topped with dulce de leche. Closer to home in Wales, they
are served with butter and jam or a slice of Caerphilly cheese.

MAKES ABOUT 12

250g plain flour
1 tsp baking powder
¼ tsp freshly grated nutmeg
¼ tsp salt
1 tsp allspice
75g caster sugar
zest of 1 lemon
50g butter, diced
50g lard or vegetable shortening, diced
1 egg
100ml milk
½ tsp vanilla extract
75g currants

Sift the flour, baking powder, grated nutmeg, salt and allspice into a bowl. Add the sugar and lemon zest and stir them into the flour. Using your fingers, work in the butter and lard or shortening until the mixture is the texture of breadcrumbs.

Beat the egg into the milk and add the vanilla. Add the egg mixture to the flour and mix to make a soft dough, then stir in the currents – this will start to look spottier than a Dalmatian with acne.

Cook the cakes on a griddle if you have one or in a heavy frying pan. Grease the pan and heat it to a medium temperature – don't let it get too hot or the outside of the cakes will burn, leaving the middles uncooked. With wet hands, or a wet spoon, take golf-ball sized pieces of the dough and flatten them to form cakes about 1cm thick. Cook for about 5 minutes on each side over a low heat.

Serve warm with butter and jam – maybe with some clotted cream on the side.

THE BRADFORD CURRY PROJECT
MUTTAR PANEER

The stated mission of the Bradford Curry Project is to provide free meals for the homeless, poor and underprivileged people of Bradford. The project was launched 17 years ago by Lashman Singh, who started out serving food from a van, and it became a charity in 1995. It is a multi-faith, multi-cultural charity in which all the major faiths of Bradford work together to serve those in need. Why is it called the Curry Project? Because in Asian communities the word 'curry' is a common denominator for food. But just as a soup kitchen doesn't only hand out soup, the Bradford Curry Project doesn't just make curry.

The Bradford Curry Project gave us this great recipe. Muttar paneer is a fresh, lightly spiced curry made with home-made Indian curd cheese (paneer) and frozen peas. It's good for vegetarians and you can vary the vegetables – for example, use half peas and half spinach. The cheese needs to be made in advance but it's easy and once that's done the curry is quick to assemble and cook. It can be frozen.

SERVES 4–6

PANEER
2 litres whole milk
2–4 tbsp lemon juice

CURRY
3 tbsp vegetable oil, for frying
1½ tsp cumin seeds
1 large onion, peeled and thinly sliced
1½ tbsp chopped garlic (6–8 large cloves)
thumb-sized piece of fresh ginger
(about 15g), chopped
red chilli or 1 tsp chilli flakes
(more if you like hot curry)
2 tsp ground coriander
750g frozen peas
10–12 cherry tomatoes, halved
(optional but they add some colour)
1–2 tsp garam masala
4 tbsp double cream or 6 tbsp milk
1–2 tbsp chopped fresh coriander
1–2 tsp lemon juice
salt to taste

First make the paneer – you will need a sieve, large bowl or saucepan, and a piece of muslin (or other thin material) for draining the cheese. Pour the milk into a heavy-based pan and slowly bring it to the boil. Once the milk starts to boil and rise up, add the lemon juice and stir with a wooden spoon. The milk will begin to curdle and separate into pale yellow liquid and small white solids (the curds). This should happen within a minute or so. If not, add some more lemon juice and keep stirring. Remove the pan from the heat.

Line a large sieve with the muslin and place it over a large bowl or saucepan. Pour the contents of the pan into the lined sieve and run some cold water through it. Tie the cloth and hang it from the tap over the sink to allow the excess water to drain away for 10 minutes. Then, keeping it fairly tightly wrapped, place the paneer on a board and put a heavy weight on top of it – this could be a pan filled with water.

Leave for at least 30–40 minutes until the paneer feels firm. The longer you can leave it, the better, but it can be used after 40 minutes. For this recipe, cut the paneer into cubes. You can fry the cheese gently in some sunflower oil to give it a crispy texture, but this is not essential.

To make the curry, heat the oil in a heavy-based pan. Add the cumin seeds and sizzle until you can smell the cumin. Add the thinly sliced onions and sauté gently until they have softened and coloured, without burning, for about 10 minutes.

Be patient, it will happen. Add the garlic, ginger and chilli and cook for about a minute. Add the coriander and salt.

Stir in the peas and the tomatoes (if using), then add a splash of water and bring to a gentle boil for about 3 minutes. Add the paneer, garam masala, cream or milk and cook for a few more minutes until everything is combined. Sprinkle on the fresh coriander and the lemon juice. Serve with Indian breads or rice.

Sunday dinners

MUSHROOM RISOTTO

Peter Polledri came along with his mum, Susan, and cooked a risotto for us. His mum is English, but Peter's family on his father's side came to London from Italy before the Second World War and started a chain of Italian cafés. Peter loves cooking and makes a mixture of Italian classics and hearty British dishes that he's learned from his mum. Peter cooks his risotto with home-made chicken broth, then uses the chicken cooked in the broth to make a chicken pie.

SERVES 4

30g dried porcini mushrooms
1 litre chicken or vegetable stock
2 tbsp olive oil
4 shallots, peeled and finely chopped
350g risotto rice
1 glass of dry white wine
2 tbsp butter
200g chestnut mushrooms, washed and sliced
2 tbsp crème fraîche or sour cream
50g Parmesan cheese, grated
salt and black pepper

Put the dried porcini mushrooms in a bowl, cover with warm water and leave them to soak for 20 minutes. Drain and chop the porcini and set aside. You can add the soaking water to the stock, but make sure you strain it well to remove any grit.

Bring the stock to the boil and keep it simmering on the hob. Heat a tablespoon of the olive oil in a high-sided pan and sweat the shallots until they are softened and translucent. Add the rice, stir well and cook for a minute or so, then pour in the wine. Stir as this sizzles and bubbles. Once the wine has evaporated, start adding the simmering stock a ladleful at a time. Wait until each ladleful has been absorbed by the rice before adding another and keep stirring. Continue until the rice is cooked – this will probably take about 20 minutes.

Meanwhile, heat a tablespoon of butter and the rest of the oil in a frying pan and sauté the chestnut mushrooms and the porcini. When the rice is ready, take the pan off the heat and stir in the mushrooms and add the cream, Parmesan and the rest of the butter. Season to taste, but take care with the salt as the stock may be quite salty. Garnish with some extra shavings of Parmesan if you like.

ROAST BEEF & YORKSHIRE PUDDING

Roast beef – England's finest and we think that the best is the standing rib roast. Fatty meat like this gives you the best flavour and beef, like lamb, is always best on the bone – viva la T-bone! Go to a good supplier and buy the best beef you can afford. Always bring the meat to room temperature before roasting and use a meat thermometer so you can get the joint roasted exactly as you want. Leave the meat to rest before carving and tip any juices into your gravy pan. Serve with roast potatoes and creamed horseradish (see page 154) and whatever vegetables are in season.

SERVES 10–12

1 x 5kg standing rib of beef, French trimmed
1 tbsp vegetable oil
1 tbsp English mustard powder
1 tbsp sea salt flakes
1 tbsp cracked black pepper
2 onions, cut in half
2 carrots or other root veg, peeled and cut into chunks
1 glass of red wine
1 dsrtsp cornflour
500ml beef stock, for gravy

Cooking times
Rare: 20 mins per kg
Medium rare: 25 mins per kg
Medium: 30 mins per kg
Well done: 40 mins per kg

Preheat the oven to 220°C/Gas 7. Warm a large frying pan on top of the stove until it is searing hot. Rub the beef with the vegetable oil, place it in the frying pan and brown it all over. Remove it from the pan and set it aside. Mix the mustard with the salt and pepper and rub it into the seared joint.

Put the onions and carrots in a roasting tin and place the seasoned meat on top. Pour some water into the tin to a depth of about 5mm – this will stop the beef from drying out and will also help make lots of lovely juices for the gravy. Put the meat into the preheated oven and cook at 220°C/Gas 7 for the first 30 minutes. Turn the oven down to 160°C/Gas 2–3 for the rest of the cooking time.

We think medium rare is the perfect way to serve a rib roast and to achieve this the core temperature of the meat must be 50°C. To check, use a meat thermometer, placing the spike into the centre of the meat. The meat is ready when the reading is 10 degrees below the desired temperature (see opposite), so for medium-rare meat, take the joint out of the oven when the temperature is 40°C. Then set it aside to rest somewhere warm for 15 minutes. During the resting time, the meat will continue to cook inside so it will reach the required temperature within the 15 minutes.

While the meat is resting, make gravy from the juices. Pour away some of the fat, put the roasting pan on the hob and add a glass of red wine. Let it bubble away for a minute or two to boil off the alcohol. Mix the cornflour with 2 tablespoons of the beef stock to make a paste. Add the rest of the stock to the pan, then stir in the cornflour paste to thicken. Mash in the veg and add any juices from the meat. Strain before serving.

YORKSHIRE PUDDING

This is Dave's mam's recipe. Dave learned to cook this when he was six years old and it always works.
Put the spoon in the bag and take out as much flour as you can load onto a tablespoon.

4 heaped tbsp flour
½ tsp salt
2 eggs, beaten
275ml full-fat milk
2 tbsp vegetable oil, such as sunflower oil, or a blob of goose fat

Sift the flour with the salt into a bowl. Make a well in the centre and gradually work in the beaten eggs. Then whisk in the milk, until the mixture resembles single cream. Leave the batter to stand for at least an hour.

Meanwhile, put the oil or goose fat in a Yorkshire pudding tin and get it smoking hot in a 200°C/Gas 6 oven. Give the batter a stir, quickly pour into the tin and watch it sizzle – this is a good thing! Bake for about 30 minutes or until it has risen to golden-brown perfection. If you're making individual puddings, cook for 10–15 minutes.

TOAD IN THE HOLE

Dave's mam used to make this with tomato sausages
so you got great red fat trails in the Yorkshire pudding.

4 good pork sausages
Yorkshire pudding batter as above

First of all, part-cook the sausages. Put them in a preheated oven at 180°C/Gas 4 and cook until browned and just cooked through. This can be done in advance.

Preheat the oven to 200°C/Gas 6. Make the Yorkshire batter as above and once you've poured it into the sizzling fat, drop in the sausages, spacing them evenly. Bake for about 30 minutes or until beautifully risen and golden and serve with gravy of any kind.

BEST-EVER ROAST POTATOES

Adding semolina is a tip we learned in Ireland and goose fat is a must for really crispy roasties. These really are the tastiest roast potatoes ever.

SERVES 4–6

1.5kg good spuds
(Maris Pipers are good for roasting)
100g goose fat
2 tbsp semolina
sea salt and black pepper

Peel the potatoes and cut them into chunks – whatever size you fancy, according to how you like your roasties.

Put them in a saucepan of cold, salted water, bring to the boil and boil for about 5 minutes. Drain well and then put the potatoes back in the saucepan and shake them to scuff up the surfaces. This helps to give you lovely crispy potatoes.

Meanwhile, preheat the oven to 200–220°C/Gas 6–7 and melt the goose fat in a roasting tin. Sprinkle the semolina over the potatoes and carefully tip them into the sizzling goose fat. Season liberally and roast until golden – this will take about 45–50 minutes, depending on the size of the potatoes.

HORSERADISH SAUCE

No roast beef dinner is complete without this!

4 tbsp grated horseradish root
1 tbsp white wine vinegar
pinch of English mustard powder
1 teaspoon caster sugar
150ml double cream
salt and black pepper

Mix all the ingredients together, season with salt and pepper to taste and serve with the beef.

APPLE & BLACKBERRY CRUMBLE

Everyone likes a good crumble! Using eating apples and Bramleys gives a lovely depth of flavour.

SERVES 6

FILLING

3 eating apples, peeled,
quartered and cored
2 Bramley cooking apples, peeled,
quartered and cored
2 tsp cinnamon
100g demerara sugar
300g blackberries

CRUMBLE TOPPING

175g plain flour
1 tsp cinnamon
140g soft brown sugar
35g porridge oats
180g cold unsalted butter

Put the quartered apples in a bowl and shuffle them around to mix them up a bit. Mix the cinnamon with the sugar in a separate bowl. Put half the apples in an oven dish and sprinkle with a third of the sugar mixture. Add the blackberries and sprinkle with the second third of sugar mixture. Cover with the remaining apples and add the remaining sugar and cinnamon mixture.

Now make the crumble topping. Put the flour and cinnamon in a bowl and mix well, then stir in the sugar and the oats. Cut the butter into small cubes, add to the mixture and rub it in with your fingertips until the mixture is the texture of breadcrumbs. Lay the crumble mixture on top of the fruit.

Preheat the oven to 170°C/Gas 3 and bake the crumble for about 40 minutes. Keep an eye on the top. If the sugar goes golden it looks great – if it turns black, not so good. Serve with home-made custard.

HOME-MADE CUSTARD

An old-fashioned treat that is definitely worth the effort. Sorry – custard powder can't compete with this.

SERVES 6

600ml whole milk
1 vanilla pod
6 large egg yolks
75g caster sugar

Pour the milk into a saucepan. Slash the vanilla pod and scrape out the seeds. Add the seeds to the cold milk and throw in the pod. Heat the milk up to boiling point, remove from the heat and leave to infuse for 15 minutes. Beat the egg yolks with the sugar until they are a pale golden colour.

Remove the vanilla pod from the milk and place the milk back on the heat. Gradually stir in the egg yolk and sugar mixture and cook until thickened. If it goes lumpy, don't despair – just pour it through a sieve. May be eaten hot or cold.

LEMON MERINGUE PIE

A pudding that everyone loves and everyone eats. Make it and enjoy yourself.

SERVES 6

PASTRY
200g plain flour
½ tsp caster sugar
125g butter, cut into cubes
1 medium free-range egg, beaten

LEMON FILLING
50g cornflour
350ml cold water
200g caster sugar
freshly squeezed juice and finely grated
zest of 4 large lemons
3 medium free-range egg yolks
1 medium free-range egg

MERINGUE TOPPING
3 medium free-range egg whites
175g caster sugar
¼ tsp vanilla extract

To make the pastry, put the flour, sugar and butter in a food processor and pulse until the mixture resembles fine breadcrumbs. With the motor running, gradually add the beaten egg and blend until the mixture forms a ball. Do not over blend or the pastry will be tough. Tip the dough onto a floured board and roll out to about 5mm thick, turning the pastry and flouring the surface regularly. Use the pastry to line a 20cm fluted flan tin. Trim the edges of the pastry neatly and chill for 30 minutes. Preheat the oven to 200°C/Gas 6.

While the pastry is resting, make the filling. Put the cornflour in a bowl and mix with enough of the cold water to make a thin paste. Set aside. Pour the remaining water into a large saucepan and add the sugar, lemon zest and juice – you should have about 225ml of lemon juice. Heat gently until the sugar dissolves, then bring to the boil. Reduce the heat slightly, then stir in the cornflour and the mixture should start to thicken.

Stir over a low heat for 3 minutes until the mixture is thick and glossy. Remove from the heat and cool for 5 minutes. Whisk the egg yolks with the whole egg until smooth, then whisk vigorously into the mixture. Set aside to cool for 25 minutes.

Put the flan tin with the pastry on a sturdy baking sheet and line with baking parchment. Fill with baking beans and bake blind in the preheated oven for 15 minutes. Carefully take it out of the oven and remove the paper and beans. Return the pastry to the oven for another 3–4 minutes until the surface is dry. Remove from the oven and reduce the temperature to 150°C/Gas 2.

To make the meringue, whisk the egg whites in a large bowl until stiff, then gradually whisk in half the sugar. Add the vanilla extract and continue whisking in the remaining sugar until it is all used. Stir the cooled lemon filling well and pour it into the pastry case. Very gently, spoon the meringue onto the top of the pie and swirl into peaks. Bake for 25 minutes at 150°C/Gas 2 or until the meringue is set and very lightly browned. Leave to cool before removing from the tin and devouring!

TEXAS CORNBREAD

Julia Vinson lives in Pakenham, Suffolk. Her mother is English, but her dad is a Texan and she's married to a man from Oklahoma who's of Cherokee descent. Julia cooked us a brilliant Sunday lunch that really made us smile and brought a true touch of Americana to Suffolk. There's a family battle over the cornbread, as both dad and husband Tony say their recipe is the best. We think the Southern cornbread is a great accompaniment, but the Texas version (pictured) is a meal in itself. Julia gets all her ingredients from the American store on the air base near where she lives, but you can buy cornmeal in the UK.

SERVES 6–8

150g yellow cornmeal
½ tsp bicarbonate of soda
1 tsp salt
240ml buttermilk
1 x 400g can of creamed corn
2 large eggs
50g bacon drippings or butter

FILLING
1 tsp vegetable oil
450g minced beef or other meat
2 onions, peeled and chopped
225g hard cheese, grated
50g jalapeño peppers, chopped

Preheat the oven 180°C/Gas 4. In a large bowl, mix the cornmeal with the bicarb and salt. Add the buttermilk, creamed corn and eggs, then beat until the batter is smooth and set aside. Put the bacon drippings or butter into a heavy pan or baking dish and place in the oven to heat up.

To make the filling, heat the oil in a frying pan and lightly brown the minced beef and the chopped onions. Pour half the batter into the hot dish and sprinkle on the browned beef and onion, cheese and jalapeños (add more if you like your food really hot), then top with the remaining batter. Bake for 45–50 minutes.

SOUTHERN CORNBREAD

SERVES 6–8

1½ tbsp melted butter
225g white cornmeal
1 tsp salt
1 tsp bicarbonate of soda
2 eggs, well beaten
480ml buttermilk

Preheat the oven 180°C/Gas 4. Add the melted butter to a heavy pan or baking dish and put the dish in the oven to heat up.

Sift the cornmeal, salt and bicarbonate of soda into a bowl. Mix the eggs with the buttermilk and stir into the cornmeal to make a smooth batter. Take the hot dish out of the oven, stir the hot butter so the sides of the pan are coated, then carefully pour the batter into the dish. Bake for 30 minutes.

PORK BBQ RIBS
& BOSTON BAKED BEANS

More from Julia. If you want to cook spare ribs and beans for a Sunday lunch in the garden, look no further than this recipe. The marinade is fantastic and the ribs are great cooked on the barbecue or in the oven. Sure to tickle a Texan.

SERVES 6

1 rack of pork ribs
3 tomatoes, chopped (plum tomatoes are best for this)
1 red onion, finely chopped
1 tsp Worcestershire sauce
1 garlic clove
1 tsp ground mustard
240ml ketchup
2 tbsp soy sauce
55g sugar
1 tbsp cornflour mixed with 3–4 tbsp of water
salt and pepper

BOSTON BAKED BEANS

400g navy or pinto beans
500g smoked streaky bacon
1 onion, peeled and finely diced
2 garlic cloves, peeled and finely diced
3 tbsp molasses
1 tsp salt
¼ tsp ground black pepper
80ml American mustard
120ml tomato ketchup
1 tbsp Worcestershire sauce
3 tbsp tomato paste
35g brown sugar

Clean the ribs and pat them dry. Slice to separate and place in a pan of boiling water for 3–5 minutes. Leave to cool.

To make the marinade, mix all the remaining ingredients, except the cornflour, in a pan and bring to boil. Once boiling, slowly stir in the cornflour mixture until the marinade has thickened, then pour it into a bowl. Add the ribs and leave them to marinate for at least 1 hour, preferably 2.

When you're ready to cook, transfer the ribs to a shallow pan and cook them in a preheated oven at 150°C/Gas 2 for 1 hour or wrap the ribs in foil and cook them on the barbecue. Timing will depend on the temperature of the grill so keep a close eye on the ribs.

BOSTON BAKED BEANS

Soak the beans overnight in cold water. The next day, bring them to the boil in the same water and simmer for 1–2 hours until tender. Drain and reserve the liquid.

Preheat the oven to 170°C/Gas 3. Chop two-thirds of the bacon into strips about 5cm long. Pour the beans into a large 2-litre pot or casserole dish and mix in the bacon strips, diced onion and garlic. Mix all the remaining ingredients in a saucepan and bring to the boil. Add some of the bean water to the mixture to give it a pouring consistency and then pour it over the beans.

Lay the remaining rashers of bacon on top of the beans and cover the dish with a lid or a piece of foil. Bake for 2 hours in the preheated oven. Check about halfway through cooking and add more liquid if the beans are getting too dry. Take off the lid 15 minutes before the end of cooking to crisp the bacon.

BUTTERMILK PIE

An American classic, this pie made a perfect end to our Sunday lunch with Julia.
It's a family favourite and Julia told us that at one time her mum wouldn't eat any American
food – except for this buttermilk pie, which her great-aunt used to make for her!

SERVES 6–8

1 unbaked pastry case or a packet of
shortcrust pastry
110g butter
150g sugar
5 eggs
240ml buttermilk
1 tsp vanilla extract
2 tbsp plain flour
juice and grated zest of ½ lemon

If you've made your own pastry or you are using a packet of bought pastry instead of a prepared pastry case, put the dough onto a floured board and roll it out to around 5mm thick, turning the pastry and flouring the surface regularly. Use it to a line a 20cm fluted flan tin. Trim the edges neatly, prick the base lightly with a fork and chill the pastry for 30 minutes. Preheat the oven to 230°C/Gas 8.

Cream the butter and sugar together until light and fluffy, then beat in the eggs one at a time. Add the remaining ingredients and pour the mixture into the unbaked pastry shell. Bake at 230°C/Gas 8 for 10 minutes, then reduce the heat to 180°C/Gas 4 and bake for a further 40 minutes until the filling is firm.

Serve with cream, ice cream or fresh fruit.

KEY LIME PIE

This is usually made in a deep pastry or biscuit crust case but can be made in a wider shallow one if you prefer. Fresh berries are often served with this traditional American dessert – blueberries are particularly good. Lots of lightly whipped cream is good too, but miss this out if you prefer.

SERVES 8

BISCUIT CRUST

175g digestive biscuits or
half digestives and half Oreo cookies
80g butter
50g sugar

FILLING

3 large free-range/organic eggs, separated
finely grated zest of 2 limes
125ml lime juice
1 x 210ml can of condensed milk
½ tsp vanilla extract
½ tsp cream of tartar
pinch of salt
80g caster sugar

Crush the biscuits with a rolling pin or in a food processor. Melt the butter in a saucepan and add the biscuit crumbs and sugar. Mix everything together well, then spread over the base of a 23cm flan tin or ceramic dish. Mould some of the mixture up the sides of the dish.

Preheat the oven to 180°C/Gas 4. Whisk the egg yolks until pale and fluffy. Beat the lime zest, juice and condensed milk together until thick and smooth, then mix with the beaten egg yolks. Spoon the filling into the biscuit case.

Whisk the egg whites until they form soft peaks. Fold in the vanilla extract, cream of tartar and salt. Then whisk in the caster sugar, a little at a time, and whisk until firm and glossy. Spoon the meringue over the filling. Use a fork to lift the surface into peaks, then bake the pie in the preheated oven for 15–20 minutes until light golden brown.

Leave to cool, then chill in the fridge before serving with blueberries and cream as desired.

BREAD & BUTTER PUDDING

**A great Sunday dinner treat. Dave's mam also had another version –
she used to spread each slice of bread with some marmalade. Delicious.**

SERVES 6

8 thick slices of white bread, ideally
taken from an unsliced sandwich loaf
75g butter, softened,
plus extra for greasing
freshly grated nutmeg
150g caster sugar,
plus 4 tbsp for sprinkling
4 large free-range egg yolks
2 large free-range eggs
300ml double cream
300ml whole milk
1 tsp vanilla extract
100g mixed dried fruit

Cut the crusts off the bread. Put the bread on a tray, cover
with a clean tea towel and leave for 3–4 hours until slightly
dried. (Partly drying the bread helps it absorb the custard.)

Spread one side of each slice of bread with softened butter
and sprinkle with a generous grating of nutmeg. Keep 4 slices
of bread whole and cut the remaining 4 into triangles. To
make the custard, whisk the sugar, egg yolks and whole eggs
together in a large bowl until smooth. Whisk in the cream,
milk and vanilla extract.

Butter a 1.75 litre ovenproof dish – a lasagne dish is ideal.
Line the dish with the whole slices of bread in one layer,
butter side up, and scatter over three-quarters of the mixed
dried fruit. Arrange the triangles on top, butter-side up and
almost standing vertically. Sprinkle the remaining fruit
between the triangles as you go.

Give the custard a stir, then pour it slowly over the bread.
The bread will float, so press it down gently for a few seconds
to help it absorb the custard. Leave to stand for 30 minutes.
Preheat the oven to 180°C/Gas 4.

Place the dish in a roasting tin. Pour in enough just-boiled
water to come halfway up the sides of the dish. Bake for
30 minutes or until the custard is just set and the bread is
golden brown and crisp on top. Carefully remove the tin
from the oven and lift out the pudding. Serve hot with cream
or good vanilla ice cream.

SMOKED EEL &
PANCETTA SALAD

Susan Burningham and her daughter Leonie Stockdale cooked us some amazing food, including this salad. Susan's mum was a cook at a stately home and she has great memories of her mother's skills. Leonie also loves cooking and is enjoying learning to make some of her mother's and grandmother's recipes. The celeriac part of this salad also goes well with smoked trout or smoked salmon, but do try the eel. It is expensive but a little goes a long way.

SERVES 12

24 paper-thin slices of pancetta or
smoked back bacon
1 smoked eel
1 medium celeriac
1 white onion
1 bunch of flat-leaf parsley
125ml single cream (or crème fraîche)
4 unwaxed lemons
walnut oil
4 bunches of fresh watercress (not
pre-packed)
freshly ground black pepper
sea salt

Preheat the oven to 200°C/Gas 6. Put the pancetta or back bacon on a roasting tray and bake on a high shelf in the oven until the bacon is crisp. Remove and place on kitchen paper to cool and drain. Set aside.

Cut the eel into slices measuring about 7.5 x 2.5cm and set aside in a cool place. Peel and grate the celeriac and the onion. Finely chop the parsley. Mix the grated vegetables with the cream and parsley, then season with black pepper and sea salt. Spoon the vegetable and cream mixture onto plates and arrange the pieces of eel and bacon on top.

Grate the zest of 2 of the lemons and squeeze the juice of one. Make a light vinaigrette with the lemon juice and walnut oil. Before serving, lightly drizzle some vinaigrette over each serving and scatter on grated lemon zest. Wash the watercress carefully and use it to garnish the plates. Add the remaining lemons cut into slices.

TURBOT
WITH SHRIMP SAUCE

Another recipe from Susan and Leonie. Turbot is the king of fish and this dish is fit for a king. Turbot can weigh up to 12kg and be a metre long, but the smaller variety is known as chicken turbot.

SERVES 12

2 chicken turbot, cleaned
about 1.2 litres milk, plus enough water
to cover each fish
1 lemon, sliced
2 tbsp chopped flat-leaf parsley

SAUCE
600ml shrimps
2 tsp plain white flour
350g unsalted butter, diced
2 pinches of ground mace
2 pinches of cayenne pepper
salt and white pepper to taste

First prepare the sauce. Peel the shrimps and set them aside. Put the shells in a pan with 900ml of water, cover, bring to the boil and simmer for 20 minutes. Strain the liquid into a measuring jug. You should have about 600ml, but if necessary, add a little water or pour the stock back into the pan and simmer again to reduce. Allow to cool slightly.

Gradually add this stock to the flour in a bowl, stirring to make a smooth sauce – the sauce should have a pouring consistency and not look like glue! Pour the sauce into a clean saucepan and add the diced butter. Stir the sauce over a moderate heat so that it thickens without boiling. Add the mace and cayenne, then season with salt and white pepper to taste. Set aside.

Score the cleaned fish through to the backbone on the dark-skinned side and place them in separate pans on top of the stove. Pour in a mixture of milk and water to cover and add the slices of lemon. Bring to a simmer and cook gently for 10–15 minutes or so. To test whether the fish is cooked, pierce the thickest part with a sharp knife. The fish should be opaque right down to the bone.

Once the fish are cooked, carefully lift them out and place on a large serving dish. Garnish with chopped parsley and a couple of tablespoons of the shrimps. Add the remaining shrimps to the sauce and warm it through gently (do not boil) before serving.

If you are cooking for a smaller number and don't want to use whole fish, you can make this dish with poached or grilled turbot fillets, or other white fish, as pictured.

ROAST SADDLE OF VENISON

A feast of a dish from Susan's mum's country house repertoire. This is a classic way of feeding a crowd and perfect for a New Year's Eve party. The venison really does need to marinate for two days, so don't skip this step.

SERVES 12

1 saddle of venison
8 streaky bacon rashers
bay leaves (optional)
120ml port wine
a knob of kneaded unsalted butter

MARINADE
300ml red wine
300ml red wine vinegar
300ml water
1 sprig of thyme
6 juniper berries, crushed
2 bay leaves, crumbled
1 blade of mace, crumbled, or ½ tsp ground mace
1 x 2.5cm strip of orange peel, white pith removed
2 star anise, crushed
sea salt
freshly ground black pepper

Use a very sharp knife to trim away any hard skin from the venison, taking care not to tear the flesh. Put the meat into a dish that almost encloses it.

Combine all the ingredients for the marinade and pour the mixture over the meat. Add a little more water if necessary in order to cover the saddle. Don't put a lid on the dish, but cover it with a piece of loosely woven cloth, such as muslin, to keep off the flies and dust. Clingfilm will do, but puncture it in a few places to allow the liquid to breathe. Leave the meat in a cool place for 2 days, turning it from time to time.

At the end of the marinating time, drain the joint (reserving the marinade) and pat it dry with kitchen paper. Preheat the oven to 200°C/Gas 6. Lay the bacon rashers across the top of the saddle and tie them in place with string – this stops the rashers curling during cooking. Add some bay leaves if you like. Place the venison saddle in a roasting tin and cover with a sheet of foil. Cook in the preheated oven for 30 minutes to seal the meat.

Add the port wine to the roasting tin and turn the oven down to 180°C/Gas 4. Continue cooking for another 45–60 minutes. Every 15 minutes, lift the foil and baste the meat with the port and some of the marinade to stop the meat drying out.

Ten minutes before the end of the cooking time, remove the foil and bacon rashers – keep the bacon warm for the garnish. Turn the oven up to 200°C/Gas 6 for 10 minutes to brown the meat.

Take the venison out of the oven, remove it from the roasting tin and keep it warm while you make the sauce. Place the roasting tin on the hob and add enough boiling water to the meat juices in the roasting tin to make up about 300ml of liquid. Stir over a high heat and gently thicken with the kneaded butter. The sauce should not be too thick. Carve the venison and garnish with the crispy bacon.

Strain the sauce and serve it separately. Redcurrant jelly and game chips are perfect accompaniments, plus a selection of fresh vegetables.

GAME CHIPS

These very thinly sliced, deep-fried potatoes are a traditional accompaniment to venison. You can make parsnip, beetroot and celeriac crisps the same way and they all go well with game.

SERVES 6

6 large potatoes
vegetable oil, for deep frying
salt and black pepper

Peel the potatoes and slice them as thinly as you can – a mandolin is great for this. Rinse the slices in cold water to remove excess starch, then drain and dry thoroughly on some kitchen paper.

Half fill a large saucepan or deep-fat fryer with oil and heat to 190°C or use an electric deep-fat fryer. Fry the potatoes a handful at time – don't crowd the pan or they won't turn crisp and golden. Season with salt and black pepper and serve as soon as possible.

STEAK & ALE PIE

Beef and beer – a classic combination made even tastier by a topping of good puff pastry.

SERVES 6

4–5 tbsp sunflower oil
200g smoked streaky bacon rashers, cut into 1cm strips
2 medium onions, peeled, halved and sliced
2 garlic cloves, peeled and finely chopped
850g well-marbled braising steak, trimmed of thick fat and gristle
500ml bottle of real ale
500ml good beef stock
1 tbsp tomato purée
3–4 sprigs of fresh thyme, leaves stripped from the stalks
2 bay leaves
250g small chestnut mushrooms, wiped and halved or quartered if large
2 tbsp cornflour
500g ready-made puff pastry
beaten egg, to glaze
sea salt and freshly ground black pepper

Heat 1 tablespoon of the oil in a large non-stick frying pan. Fry the bacon strips with the onions until pale golden brown, stirring regularly. Add the garlic and fry for a minute or two until softened. Using a slotted spoon, transfer the onions, garlic and bacon to a large flame-proof casserole dish.

Cut the steak into rough 2.5cm cubes and season with salt and pepper. Heat 2 tablespoons of oil in the frying pan and fry the meat over a medium heat in 2 or 3 batches until well browned all over. Add extra oil if the pan seems dry. Transfer the beef to the casserole dish as it is browned.

Preheat the oven to 180°C/Gas 4. Deglaze the frying pan with half the ale. Bring it to the boil while stirring hard to lift all the sediment from the bottom of the pan. Pour this over the beef. Add the remaining ale, then the stock, tomato purée and herbs to the dish. Bring everything to the boil, then cover and cook in the oven for 1½–2 hours or until the meat is very tender. Mix the cornflour with 2 tablespoons of cold water until smooth and stir into the casserole. Put the dish back in the oven for a further 5 minutes or until the juices are thick. Adjust the seasoning to taste and leave to cool.

Turn the oven up to 200°C/Gas 6. Place a pastry funnel in the centre of a 1.2 litre pie dish. Heat the remaining oil in a frying pan and fry the mushrooms over a high heat for about 5 minutes until golden, then add them to the meat. Spoon everything into the pie dish around the funnel.

Roll out the puff pastry on a well-floured board. Brush the edge of the dish with beaten egg. Make a small cross in the centre of the pastry for the top of the pie funnel to poke through. Place the pastry gently over the filling and funnel. Press the edges firmly to seal and trim neatly, then flute them or leave plain, as you prefer. Decorate the top with any excess pastry and brush with more beaten egg to glaze. Place the dish on a baking sheet and bake in the centre of the oven for 30–35 minutes until puffed up and golden brown.

PERFECT
CAULIFLOWER CHEESE

**Dave's mam's recipe for a really satisfying cauliflower cheese. Serve with meat
or by itself as a great vegetarian supper dish. Good with some crusty bread.**

SERVES 4

1 large cauliflower, big as a gorilla's head
2 tbsp olive oil
250g chestnut mushrooms, wiped and
finely sliced
25g butter
2 tbsp plain flour
250ml whole milk
½ tsp English mustard powder
200g Gruyère cheese, grated
pinch of nutmeg, freshly grated
50g ciabatta breadcrumbs
50g Parmesan cheese, finely grated
salt and black pepper to taste

Trim the cauliflower and break it into florets. Bring a big saucepan of water to the boil, add the florets and boil for about 10 minutes until just soft. Drain and set aside. While this is happening…

Heat the oil in a frying pan and sauté the mushrooms until they are just starting to take on a bit of colour. Set aside.

Melt the butter in a saucepan and beat in the flour. Add the milk, stirring all the time, to make a thick white sauce. Add the mustard powder and grated Gruyère, while still stirring, and check the seasoning. Fold in the mushrooms.

Preheat the oven to 180°C/Gas 4. Put the cauliflower florets in an oven dish, pour in the cheesy mushroom sauce and add a sprinkling of freshly grated nutmeg. Mix the ciabatta crumbs with the grated Parmesan and spread them over the top. Place in the preheated oven and bake for about 15 minutes until the sauce is bubbling and the crumbs and Parmesan mixture is golden. Yum, yum.

RUM BABAS

Dave's mam used to make these, so did Si's. They're a real treat and well worth the effort. Don't be shy with the rum! The babas will keep for two or three days in the fridge.

SERVES 8–12

75g currants or mixed dried fruit

4 tbsp dark rum

225g plain flour

1 x 7g sachet of easy-blend dried yeast

½ tsp fine sea salt

4 large free-range eggs, beaten

4 tbsp milk

1 tbsp clear honey

115g butter, well softened but not melted, plus extra for greasing

SYRUP

400g caster sugar

4–6 tbsp dark rum

3 tbsp clear honey

Put the currants in a saucepan with the 4 tablespoons of rum and 2 tablespoons of cold water. Place over a medium heat and bring to the boil. Remove from the heat and leave to cool. Generously grease 8–10 metal rum baba moulds set on a baking tray or a deep 12-hole muffin tin.

Sift the flour into a large bowl and stir in the yeast and salt. Beat the eggs with the milk and honey. Beat the egg mixture and the butter into the dry ingredients with a wooden spoon for about 5 minutes or until very smooth and glossy. Drain the currants, reserving the rum, and stir into the batter. Spoon the mixture into the prepared moulds or tin and leave in a warm place to rise for about 30 minutes or until risen by about a quarter. Preheat the oven to 190°C/Gas 5. Bake for 12–15 minutes or until the babas are well risen and golden brown.

While the babas are baking, make the syrup. Put the sugar in a saucepan with 400ml cold water and heat gently, stirring occasionally until the sugar dissolves. Bring to a simmer and add the rum and honey, plus the rum set aside earlier. Let it bubble for a few seconds, then remove from the heat and leave to stand.

Remove the babas from the oven and cool in the moulds for 5 minutes. Loosen the sides with a blunt-ended knife and turn the babas out into a large, shallow ceramic dish. (You may need to put them on their sides, but that's fine.) Taste the syrup, taking care as it will still be hot, and add a little more rum if you like. Pour half the syrup slowly over the babas. Leave to stand for 5 minutes.

Now, carefully turn the babas over in the dish. Pour over the remaining syrup and leave the babas for a further 10 minutes. They'll be very thirsty, so don't be surprised if they soak up nearly all the syrup. Turn once more, then cover and chill in the fridge for at least 2 hours before serving. Serve with lots of double cream.

SPOTTED DICK

**Only in Britain… this is a real rib-sticking pud and we love it.
Serve with lots of home-made custard (see page 159).**

SERVES 6

150g fresh white breadcrumbs
200g self-raising flour, plus extra for
dusting
100g golden caster sugar
150g currants
115g shredded beef suet
½ tsp ground mixed spice
pinch of fine sea salt
juice and finely grated zest of 1 lemon
1 large free-range egg
75ml whole milk

Mix the breadcrumbs, flour, sugar, currants, suet, mixed spice, salt and lemon zest in a large bowl. Beat together the egg and milk and add the lemon juice. Stir into the dry ingredients until well combined. The dough should feel light and spongy. Turn out onto a floured board, knead very lightly and form into a rectangle roughly the size of a house brick.

Half fill a large saucepan with water and bring to the boil. Sprinkle flour over a large piece of clean sheeting, or a thin tea towel. (An old pillowcase can also be cut to the right size for this job.) Place the spotted dick on top and bring up the ends of the material. Leave room for the pud to expand, then tie tightly with kitchen string to seal the parcel.

Lower the pudding gently and carefully into the boiling water. Cover with a lid and boil for 1 hour, checking the water level from time to time and topping up as needed. The pudding should be well risen and cooked through at the end of the hour. Turn off the heat and lift the pudding carefully from the water using tongs. Take great care, as the water will be very hot. Put the pudding on a board and leave to cool for 3–4 minutes. Snip off the string, unwrap the spotted dick and place it on a serving dish.

Another way of cooking spotted dick is to wrap the pudding in a double thickness of pleated and buttered baking parchment tied with string and then steam it for 2 hours.

CHINESE OLDER PEOPLE'S GROUP
SWEET & SOUR PORK
HONG KONG STYLE

The Chinese Older People's Group is based in Oxford and meets every Monday to enjoy
a meal, sing karaoke and keep fit. On Thursdays, the group meets again to learn IT skills,
English and Mandarin and the members also take trips to interesting places around the
country. Anyone can join – you just have to be over 50.

This is the group's version of one of the best-known Chinese dishes.

SERVES 4

1kg pork (neck fillet or lean belly pork)
1 chicken stock cube
4 tbsp white sugar
1 egg
4 tbsp cornflour
vegetable oil, for frying
3 tbsp tomato ketchup
75ml red wine vinegar
1 x 400g can of pineapple chunks with
natural juice

Cut the pork into pieces measuring about 2.5 x 3cm and put
them in a bowl. Mix the chicken stock cube with a little water,
add 1 tablespoon of the white sugar, then season with salt and
pepper. Add this to the pork, mix well and leave to marinate
for 30 minutes.

Whisk the egg with 1 tablespoon of the cornflour and mix
this with the pork. Heat a wok, add some oil and heat until
very hot, then turn down the heat before frying.

Put 2 tablespoons of the cornflour in a bowl and use this
to coat the pieces of pork, one at a time, before frying.
Don't mix the cornflour with all the pork pieces at once.

1 tbsp Worcestershire sauce
salt and white pepper

Fry the pork for 7–8 minutes until cooked through. Then drain on kitchen paper and put to one side.

Meanwhile, mix the tomato ketchup with the vinegar, pineapple chunks and juice, Worcestershire sauce and the rest of the white sugar. Pour this into a saucepan and cook for 2 minutes. Mix the remaining tablespoon of cornflour with a little cold water and add to the sauce to thicken it.

Fry the pork pieces again for 2 minutes until golden brown and drain on kitchen paper. Mix the pork with the warm sweet and sour sauce and serve with some rice.

Picnics

STICKY GINGER & SOY CHICKEN WINGS

Yasmeen Ismail's family comes from Pakistan and Afghanistan and she now lives in Hall Green, Birmingham. Yasmeen gave us some great family recipes, including a special masala mix from her Auntie Taz, which up until now has been a closely guarded secret! One of her prized possessions is a pestle and mortar passed down from her grandmother. These chicken wings are fantastically tasty and will fly off your picnic blanket.

SERVES 4

4 tbsp dark soy sauce
1 tbsp wholegrain mustard
1 handful of finely chopped root ginger
2 tbsp oil
20 chicken wings

Mix the marinade ingredients in an ovenproof dish and add the chicken. Leave to marinate overnight for best results.

The next day, preheat the oven to 200°C/Gas 6 and roast the wings for 30 minutes until cooked through and wonderfully brown and sticky. Cook them skin down to ensure they are crispy and serve with a sweet chilli sauce.

AUNTIE TAZ'S CHAAT MASALA MIX

The Ismail family's secret recipe.

whole or flaked red chillies
cumin seeds
coriander seeds
pinch of salt
pinch of lovage seeds
pinch of citric acid powder

Put equal quantities of chillies, cumin and coriander into a pan and roast. Leave to cool and then put them into a pestle and mortar or a spice grinder. Add a pinch each of salt, lovage seeds and citric acid and grind everything together until you have a mixture with a fine consistency – the infamous Ismail masala mix is ready!

SPINACH, CARROT & POTATO PAKORAS

Yasmeen's pakoras were some of the best we've ever tasted and that's the truth.

MAKES 16 LARGE PAKORAS

250g spinach, chopped
4 carrots, grated or julienned
4 medium potatoes, thinly sliced
1 onion, peeled and sliced
250g gram (chick pea) flour
1 tsp salt
1 tsp dried red chillies
1 tsp each of cumin and lovage seeds
vegetable oil

Combine all the ingredients together and add lukewarm water to create a paste. The consistency should be firm enough for you to mould – if it's runny, it won't work.

Take a large dessertspoon of the mixture and mould with your hands.

Heat the oil in a large saucepan until very hot and add a few handfuls of the mixture. Once the pakoras are holding together, turn the heat down so they cook inside and deep fry for 4–5 minutes until golden and crispy. Serve with some mint and coriander chutney.

CHANA CHAAT

This is a spicy yoghurt salad, made extra-special by the Ismail family's masala mix (see opposite).

SERVES 4

1 x 500g tub of natural yoghurt
240ml whole milk
1 tsp salt
½ tsp dried red chillies
1 tsp masala mix
2 tomatoes, diced
½ cucumber, diced
1 red onion, peeled and chopped
1 x 400g can of chick peas
1 green chilli, finely chopped (optional)

Whisk the yoghurt and milk together until the mixture is smooth. Add the salt, chillies and masala mix and stir well. Add the tomatoes, cucumber and onions and stir in the chick peas.

For a salad with a bit more of a kick, add a finely chopped green chilli.

SCOTCH EGGS

Good old-fashioned Scotch eggs are perfect for a coach trip or a picnic. You can use this recipe as a base and get creative – how about Scotch eggs with black pudding (opposite) or smoked haddock?

SERVES 6

6 eggs
500g good sausage meat or 250g
sausage meat and 250g black pudding
½ tsp dried thyme
1 tsp dried sage
½ tsp black pepper
pinch of cayenne pepper
2 eggs, beaten
4 tbsp plain flour
125g fresh white breadcrumbs
vegetable oil, for deep frying

For eggs with a slightly runny middle, put them into cold water, bring to the boil and boil for 5 minutes. Leave to cool, then remove the shells. Meanwhile, mix the sausage meat with the thyme, sage, black pepper and cayenne and divide the mixture into 6. Flatten these portions out into thin patties and wrap one around each egg. Smooth the coating so that it is nice and even.

Put the beaten eggs, flour and breadcrumbs into separate bowls. Roll each Scotch egg in flour, dip into the beaten egg and then roll in the fresh breadcrumbs. Dip each one into the beaten egg again and roll in some more breadcrumbs to build up a good coating. Heat the oil in a large pan to about 170°C. Deep fry the Scotch eggs until golden – this will take 4–5 minutes. Drain on kitchen paper and leave to cool.

NARGIS KEBABS

This is an Indian version of Scotch eggs, rolled in a crunchy sesame seed coating.

SERVES 4

250g minced beef or lamb
2 garlic cloves, peeled and crushed
2.5cm piece of root ginger, grated
½ tsp ground coriander
½ tsp ground cumin
½ tsp chilli powder (or more to taste)
¼ tsp ground cloves
1 tbsp cornflour
salt to taste
1 egg yolk
4 hard-boiled eggs, shelled
2 tbsp flour
1 egg, beaten
2 tbsp sesame seeds
vegetable oil, for shallow-frying

Mix the meat, garlic, ginger, spices, cornflour and salt in a bowl. Bind with the egg yolk and divide the mixture into 4 equal parts.

With well-floured hands, flatten each portion into a round. Place a hard-boiled egg in the centre and carefully work the meat round it to cover.

Put the 2 tablespoons of flour, beaten egg and sesame seeds in separate bowls. Roll the nargis kebabs in flour, egg, then sesame seeds until well coated. Heat the oil in a pan and shallow fry the kebabs until brown.

COURGETTE FRITTERS

Heather Lane lives in Crawley and loves to cook from her own notebooks of recipes that she has collected over the years. She's also a keen gardener and likes to make the most of her vegetables. This recipe is a great way to use up a glut of courgettes and brings an Asian twist to a popular classic.

MAKES ABOUT 12

3 courgettes, grated

1 onion, peeled and grated

1 garlic clove, crushed

vegetable oil

100g gram (chick pea) flour

2 eggs, beaten

1 tsp garam masala

160g strong crumbly cheese, such as feta or Lancashire

1 small red or green chilli, seeded and finely chopped

small handful of mint, chopped

small handful of parsley or fresh coriander, chopped

salt and freshly ground black pepper to taste

Place the grated courgettes and onion in a colander and leave for 10–15 minutes to drain. Squeeze out any excess water and add the garlic. Heat a little vegetable oil in a frying pan and fry the courgettes, onion and crushed garlic until they are just starting to brown. Remove from the heat and allow to cool slightly.

Beat the flour with the eggs and garam masala to make a smooth batter – add a little milk if the batter seems too thick. Stir in the crumbled cheese, chilli, mint, parsley or coriander, salt and pepper and then add the cooked courgettes and onions. Stir until everything is thoroughly mixed.

Heat more oil in the frying pan and drop tablespoon-sized dollops of the mixture into the hot pan, a few at a time. Fry gently, then flip over to cook the other side. When the fritters are cooked through and golden and crispy on the outside, remove them from the pan and drain on kitchen paper.

These fritters freeze well and can be reheated in a hot oven from frozen – just make sure they are really piping hot all the way through.

VICTORIA SANDWICH

Heather's great-granny used to run a bakery in Barrow-in-Furness at the end of the 19th century and Heather recently came across a book of her recipes, all handwritten of course. This is great-granny Gawthrop's classic recipe for Victoria sandwich, which is a must for every picnic. It's so simple. You just weigh the eggs and use the same weight of butter, sugar and flour.

SERVES 10–12

For a 7in/18cm cake
weigh 4 eggs

For a 6in/15cm cake
weigh 3 eggs

butter, room temperature
caster sugar
self-raising flour, sifted
few drops of vanilla extract
pinch of baking powder
1 pot strawberry jam
icing sugar

Grease and line 2 sandwich tins. Weigh the eggs and then weigh out the same amount of butter, caster sugar, and self-raising flour. Preheat the oven to 180°C/Gas 4.

Cream the butter and sugar together and beat until light and fluffy. Beat the eggs and add to the butter and sugar a little at a time. Add a small amount of the flour at the same time to stop the mixture curdlng. Add the vanilla extract.

Gently fold in the rest of the sifted flour and baking powder with a metal tablespoon. Be very gentle at this stage. The mixture should be a soft dropping consistency. If it seems a little stiff, add a dash of milk. Divide the mixture between the sandwich tins and bake in the centre of the oven for 25–30 minutes until done. Remove the cakes from the tins and leave to cool on a wire rack. When the cakes are cool, sandwich them together with strawberry jam and sift some icing sugar over the top.

YUMMY BISCUITS

Another of Heather's recipes. You forget how nice home-made biscuits are and these are some of the best.

MAKES ABOUT 18

100g butter, room temperature
100g caster sugar
200g self-raising flour
1 tsp golden syrup

Preheat the oven to 190°C/Gas 5. Cream the butter and sugar together until light and fluffy. Add the flour and syrup and mix to a soft dough. Roll into small balls and place on greased baking trays, giving the biscuits room to spread. Press each one down slightly.

Bake for about 6–10 minutes until golden, then allow the biscuits to cool slightly before transferring them to a wire rack.

GAME PIE

These quantities make enough pastry and filling for a deep pie in a 20cm tin. Use any game you fancy but make sure you trim it all carefully. Ideal for a high-class picnic.

SERVES 4–6

CRUST

450g plain flour

2 tsp baking powder

½ tsp salt

60g cold unsalted butter, diced

60g cold lard, diced

1 egg yolk

about 120ml water

1 packet of puff pastry for the lid

FILLING

4 tbsp vegetable oil

1.5kg mixed game meat, cut into cubes

500g venison steak, cut into cubes

125g streaky bacon, diced into lardons

2 large onions, peeled and sliced

1 celery stick, sliced

250g chestnut mushrooms, wiped clean and sliced

55g plain flour

2 bay leaves

500ml red wine

1 dsrtsp chopped thyme

500ml beef stock

2 tbsp redcurrant jelly

1 egg, beaten

sea salt flakes

ground black pepper

First, make the shortcrust case. Put the flour, baking powder and salt in a food processor, add the butter, lard and egg yolk and process until the mixture forms crumbs. Gradually add the water until a ball of pastry miraculously appears. If you don't have a processor, struggle on with a basin and a spoon. Wrap the pastry in clingfilm and put it in the fridge to chill for an hour while you get on with the filling.

Heat the oil in a large frying pan and brown the game meat and venison in batches. Take care not to put too much in the pan at once – the meat needs to be sealed, not poached. As the meat is browned, remove it and set aside.

Add the bacon and onions to the same pan and cook until the onions are translucent. Add the celery and the mushrooms and cook for a further 3 minutes. Add the flour and cook for 2 minutes. Now add the bay leaves, red wine, thyme, stock and redcurrant jelly. Season well and simmer gently, uncovered, for about 2 hours or until the meat is tender and melting – exact timing depends on the meat. Leave to cool.

While the pie filling is cooling you can blind bake the pastry case. Preheat the oven to 180°C/Gas 4. Roll out the shortcrust pastry and line a well-greased pie tin. Line with baking parchment, then fill with baking beans. Place in the preheated oven for 20 minutes until the pastry is cooked. Remove and leave to cool.

Once the pastry case is cool, fill it with the cooked meat. Pack it in – a well-filled pie is a happy pie! Preheat the oven to 180°C/Gas 4. Roll out the puff pastry. Paint around the edge of the shortcrust case with the beaten egg and place the sheet of puff pastry on the top. Crimp around the edges, trim and cut a couple of holes in the top to let the steam out. Decorate the top with any excess pastry. Brush with egg and bake at 180°C/Gas 4 for about 30 minutes until golden. Leave to cool completely before serving with some pickles and a glass of wine.

HOT CHICKEN SALAD

We met Bridget Woodcock, from Oxford, with her daughter Jennie and granddaughter Georgia. Bridget was the wife of a headmaster and used to entertain a lot – she would make several main courses and five choices of puddings when people came for dinner. This recipe is one that Jennie remembers from her childhood. We weren't sure about it – until we had a taste. It's irresistible and we couldn't stop eating.

SERVES 6–8

1 large onion, chopped
1 green pepper, seeded and chopped
1 red pepper, seeded and chopped
1 yellow pepper, seeded and chopped
1 tbsp vegetable oil
500g cooked chicken, cut into cubes
250g celery, finely chopped
1 x 295g can of concentrated chicken soup
200ml mayonnaise
4 tbsp lemon juice
butter, for greasing dish
120g cheese, grated
2 packets of cheese & onion crisps, crushed
salt and pepper

Preheat the oven to 180°C/Gas 4. Gently fry the chopped onion and peppers in a little oil for a few minutes to soften. Toss them with the chicken, celery, chicken soup, mayonnaise, lemon juice and seasoning and pile into a buttered ovenproof dish.

Mix the grated cheese and crushed crisps and sprinkle over the top of the dish, then bake for 30 minutes until golden and crispy. That's it!

MARYLAND CHICKEN

Bridget used to make classic chicken Maryland, but Jennie now cooks this healthier version, which she devised. Her daughter, Georgia, prepared the bananas for us. Incidentally, Maryland chicken was on the menu of the last lunch served in the first-class dining room on the *Titanic*!

SERVES 4

4 chicken breasts, skin on
2 tbsp honey
2 garlic cloves, peeled and crushed
4 x 2mm slices of root ginger
55ml soy sauce

BACON-WRAPPED BANANAS
4 bananas, peeled
8 streaky bacon rashers

FRITTERS
110g flour
1 egg
150ml milk
1 x 340g can of sweetcorn
vegetable oil, for frying

Start by making the marinade for the chicken. Warm the honey and mix it with the garlic, ginger and soy sauce. Place the chicken in a dish and pour the marinade over it. Make sure it is well coated, turning the pieces repeatedly if necessary. Cover and leave for a couple of hours or overnight in the fridge. Fry the chicken if you like, or preheat the oven to 200°C/Gas 6 and bake the chicken for 40–45 minutes or until cooked.

Wrap the bananas with the streaky bacon and grill or bake in a hot oven, 200°C/Gas 6, until the bacon is crispy.

To make the fritters, beat the flour, egg and milk together to make a thick batter, adding a little water if necessary. Add the drained sweetcorn. Heat a little oil in a frying pan and drop in spoonfuls of the mixture. Fry until golden brown on both sides and serve with the chicken and bananas.

This is our classic version, which goes well with Jennie and Bridget's fritters and bananas. Yee ha!

SERVES 4

1 chicken, skinned and jointed on the bone, breasts cut in 2
150g flour
1 tsp salt
1 tsp paprika
½ tsp black pepper
2 eggs, beaten
500g breadcrumbs
oil, for deep frying

Dry the chicken with kitchen paper. Mix the flour, salt, paprika and pepper and put the mixture into a plastic bag. Add the chicken and toss until the portions are well covered.

Mix the beaten eggs with 1 tablespoon of water in a bowl and put the breadcrumbs in another bowl. Dip the chicken in the beaten egg, then dredge in breadcrumbs. You might need more egg, depending on the size of your chicken.

Heat the oil to about 160°C in a large pan or deep-fat fryer and fry the chicken until the breadcrumbs are golden and the chicken is absolutely cooked through.

STICKY DATE CAKE

This is a slightly bonkers story but true. A lady came up to us in a supermarket, gave us this recipe, told us to try it and said ta ta. It's odd but brilliant, and fabulous for a picnic. Keeps well, too. Wrap it in foil and store it in a tin.

SERVES AT LEAST 12

110g raisins
225g dates, chopped
175g sultanas
110g currants
275g butter, plus extra for greasing the cake tin
1 x 400g tin condensed milk
150g wholemeal flour
150g plain flour
pinch of salt
scant tsp bicarbonate of soda
1 heaped tbsp chunky marmalade
blanched almonds and glacé cherries for the top (optional)

Grease a 20cm square cake tin with a little butter and line with baking parchment.

Put the raisins, dates, sultanas and currants in a saucepan with the butter, then pour in the condensed milk and 275ml of water. Bring this to the boil, stirring frequently so the mixture doesn't stick to the bottom of the pan, and continue to simmer for 3 minutes. Pour the mixture into a large bowl and allow to cool.

Preheat the oven to 170°C/Gas 3. In another bowl, mix the wholemeal and the plain flour with the salt and bicarb. Once the fruit mixture is cool, fold it into the flour and stir in the marmalade. Spoon the mixture into the greased and lined cake tin and decorate with some whole blanched almonds and glacé cherries if you like. Put a double layer of baking parchment over the top to keep it from burning and bake in the preheated oven for 1¾ hours.

At the end of the cooking time, take the cake out of the oven and leave it to cool in the tin for 10 minutes before turning it out onto a cooling rack. Make a nice cup of tea and cut yourself a big slice.

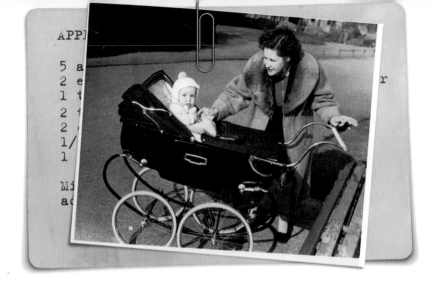

BLACKBERRY & APPLE PIE

This is a plate pie so you can take it to your picnic on the plate and be sure that it will arrive intact. The pastry recipe makes enough for top and bottom crusts on a good-sized dinner plate.

SERVES 6

PASTRY
450g plain flour
2 tsp of baking powder
½ tsp salt
60g cold unsalted butter, plus extra for greasing the plate
60g cold lard
1 egg yolk

FILLING
½ tbsp semolina
3 eating apples, peeled, quartered and cored
2 Bramley cooking apples, peeled, quartered and cored
1 dsrtsp cinnamon
100g demerara sugar
300g blackberries
1 egg, beaten
1 tbsp granulated sugar

Start by making the pastry. Put the flour, baking powder and salt in a food processor. Cut the butter and lard into cubes, add to the flour with the egg yolk and process until the mixture forms crumbs. Gradually add up to 120ml of water until a ball of pastry miraculously appears. You can, of course, do this with a basin, a spoon and your hands. Wrap the pastry in clingfilm and chill it in the fridge for an hour.

Preheat the oven to 180°C/Gas 4. Roll out half the pastry and line a buttered dinner plate. Sprinkle with the semolina to soak up excess moisture and keep the pastry crisp. Put the quartered apples in a bowl and shuffle them around to mix them up a bit. Mix the cinnamon with the sugar in a separate bowl. Put half the apples on the pastry-lined plate and sprinkle with a third of the sugar mixture. Add the blackberries and sprinkle with the second third of sugar mixture. Cover with the remaining apples and add the rest of the sugar and cinnamon.

Brush the rim of the pastry with beaten egg. Roll out the remaining pastry and put a lid on your pie. Crimp the edges, brush with egg and sprinkle with the granulated sugar. Bake in the preheated oven for about 40 minutes until the pie is golden. Serve with home-made custard (see page 159).

TREACLE TART

For those with a sweet tooth, treacle tart is the ultimate fix. It tastes great hot or cold – and it's even more delicious the next day. Serve with vanilla ice cream, custard or lashings of double cream. The name is misleading, though, as it is always made with golden syrup, not treacle.

SERVES 6

FILLING

2 large free-range eggs, beaten
1 x 454g can of golden syrup
finely grated zest of ½ small lemon
(about 1 tsp)
125g white breadcrumbs, made from a
day-old loaf

PASTRY

200g plain flour
125g cold butter, cut into cubes
1 medium free-range egg, beaten

First make the filling. Put the eggs in a large bowl and stir in the syrup – yes, the whole can. Add the lemon zest, followed by the breadcrumbs and set the mixture aside while you make the pastry. This will give the breadcrumbs time to soften and absorb the syrup.

To make the pastry, put the flour and the butter in a food processor and pulse until the mixture resembles fine breadcrumbs. With the motor running, gradually add the beaten egg and blend until the mixture forms a ball. Do not overblend or the pastry will be tough.

Tip the dough onto a floured board and roll it out to around 5mm thick, turning the pastry and flouring the surface regularly. Use it to line a 20cm loose-based cake tin – the kind used for baking a Victoria sandwich. Trim the edges neatly, prick the base lightly with a fork and chill the pastry for 30 minutes. Preheat the oven to 200°C/Gas 6.

Put the pastry case on a sturdy baking sheet and line with crumpled baking parchment. Fill with baking beans. Bake blind for 15 minutes, then carefully take it out of the oven and remove the paper and beans. Return the pastry to the oven for another 3–4 minutes until the surface is dry. Remove from the oven and reduce the temperature to 170°C/Gas 3.

Pour the syrup mixture into the tart case and smooth the surface. Bake for 25–30 minutes or until the filling is pale golden brown and set. Leave in the tin for 15 minutes before removing, then cut into generous wedges to serve.

AFRICAN & AFRICAN CARIBBEAN COMMUNITY GROUPS

Two African and African Caribbean community groups from Oxford came to our recipe fair. There's an over-50s group and a carers group and they meet every week to give each other support and take part in different activities. The over-50s cook wonderful food from African and Caribbean recipes and they run a lunch club for the many people who want to try their cooking.

CHICKEN & VEGETABLE STIR FRY

A quick, healthy meal with lots of vegetables and a great spicy taste.

SERVES 4–6

500g boneless chicken breasts
2 tbsp soy sauce
1 tsp curry powder
juice of 1 lemon
1 tsp olive oil
1 medium onion, peeled and chopped
3 medium carrots, peeled and cut into strips
½ medium-sized head of broccoli or cauliflower, trimmed and cut into small florets
handful of stringless green beans, cut into strips
3 garlic cloves, peeled and crushed
1 red and 1 yellow pepper, cored and diced
1 bag of fresh spinach
handful of fresh basil leaves, chopped
salt and pepper

Cut the chicken breasts into strips and mix them with the soy sauce. Mix the curry powder with the lemon juice to make a paste and season with salt and pepper.

Put the strips of chicken into the paste and turn them until they are well coated.

Heat the oil in a wok and add the onion and chicken and fry until cooked. Add the remaining vegetables, except the spinach, and fry for 1½ minutes.

Add the spinach and turn off the heat – the spinach will wilt down in the heat of the pan. Sprinkle with chopped basil and serve with rice or mashed potatoes.

Acknowledgments

First and foremost, we'd like to thank the mums and their families who appear in the programmes and provided recipes for this book: Aida and Victoria, Bridget, Jennie and Georgia, Connie and Charlotte, Eele, Fiona and Sybil, Gameelah, Harjinder, Heather, Ira, Jeni, Julia, Leonie and Susan, Maureen, Muriel, Susan and Peter, Tessa, Yasmeen and Yvonne. Huge thanks to you all for letting us into your homes and hearts and sharing your family culinary secrets.

At the recipe fairs we'd also like to thank the various community groups who fed and supported us – the WI, Chinese Older People's Group, the Gurkhas, the Bradford Curry Project, the West African Ghanaian Community Group, and the African and African Caribbean Community Group. Thanks must also go to more than a thousand mums and families who turned up with their treasures at our fairs. Without them none of this would have been possible. And many thanks to our new mate Gerard Baker, to Toti Gifford and his magical circus folks, and to Claire Bassano and Rupinda Ashworth.

Back at the Mailbox mothership, huge thanks to Nick Patton, head of studio BBC Birmingham, Gill Tierney, our executive producer, and editors Simon Prentice, Dan Wardle, Steve Killick and Andrew McKenzie.

Special thanks to our old friend and colleague from Hairy Baker days Oliver Clark, series producer, and our two directors François Gandolfi and Duncan Barnes – not forgetting their mums, who both sent us recipes for the book.

On the road, we'd like to thank our production manager Sarah Greene, researchers Stu Small and Leila Finikarides, and production coordinators Sarah Reddi and Rachel Holden. Also thanks to our great cameramen Roger Laxon, Will Hutchinson and Jon Boast for making us look presentable, and to our sound men Gary Goodhand, Ryan Patton, James Baker and Paul Miller. Last but not least, we owe a huge debt of gratitude to our home economist and good friend Sammy-Jo Squires. Thanks also to Max Beats, Tim Jones, Joe Barrett, Dan Slee and everyone else involved in making the programme happen.

Thanks, too, to Alan Jones and Derek Crutchlow for help with our lovely bikes.

We are very proud of this book and much credit for this must go once again to our friends at Orion. Thanks to the lovely Amanda Harris, Lucie Stericker for her skill and for letting us wreck her kitchen, Kate Barr for her gorgeous design, and Jinny Johnson for her patience and command of the English language. A huge thank you to Cristian Barnett and his assistant Martin Reftel for the fab photographs and to Sammy-Jo and her assistant Nikki Morgan for all their hard work making the food for the book. Thanks, too, to Stu Small for the great photographs he took at the fairs, Niall O'Mara for his pictures of the Ghanaian Community Group dishes, and Avril Hunter for her pictures of the Bradford Curry Project dish.

And, of course, as well as all these lovely folk, we'd like to thank our wonderful families for putting up with the pair of us.

Si & Dave

Eele

Aida & Victoria

Yvonne

Julia

Heather

Harji

Jeni

Yasmeen

Leonie